LEARN ON THE LOO

LEARN ON THE LOO

MAKING YOUR ME TIME MORE PRODUCTIVE

GRAEME DONALD

Michael O'Mara Books Limited

First published in Great Britain in 2015 by
Michael O'Mara Books Limited
9 Lion Yard
Tremadoc Road
London SW4 7NQ

A CIP catalogue record for this book is available from the British
Library.

Papers used by Michael O'Mara Books Limited are natural, recyclable
products made from wood grown in sustainable forests. The
manufacturing processes conform to the environmental regulations of
the country of origin.

ISBN: 978-1-78243-394-1 in paperback print format
ISBN: 978-1-78243-398-9 in ebook format

4 5 6 7 8 9 10

www.mombooks.com

Cover design by Dan Mogford
Designed and typeset by K DESIGN, Winscombe, Somerset

Printed and bound by CPI Group (UK) Ltd, Croydon, CR0 4YY

For Samantha June Kelly and Raffety – your strength will make dreams come true.

CONTENTS

INTRODUCTION

With most of us hostage to mobile communications, the loo is the last refuge for the mobiephobe and the only room in the house to which you can lock the door without arousing suspicion.

Such cloistered seclusion has coaxed forth great thoughts from some. Martin Luther, a lifelong sufferer of constipation, spent many a pensive hour in voluntary self-confinement with the concept of 'justification by faith' and the new Protestant movement springing from 'the knowledge the Holy Spirit gave me on the privy in the tower'. More recently, in an interview in March 2015, Sir Paul McCartney revealed the secret of his song-writing success – he always retires to the loo for inspiration and solitude. His advice to anyone seeking success: 'Go into the toilet; toilets are good. Separate yourself.' Perhaps of the same opinion, Richard Berry famously penned the first version of the classic song 'Louie Louie' on loo paper.

Now then, I'm not saying that reading this book will spur any reader to start a new branch of Christianity or launch them to superstardom, but some of the snippets in the following pages might act as teasing springboards and encourage you to look deeper into a variety of subjects. And who knows where that may take you?

IT'S A WILD WORLD: SECRETS OF THE ANIMAL KINGDOM

EVOLUTIONARY ODDITIES

- All female marsupials have at least two vaginas and two uteri, while the males come equipped with a double penis.

- A flamingo's long neck is essential as it can only eat with its head upside down.

- The common housefly beats 345 strokes of its wings a second, which creates a hum in the key of F.

- When she goes into heat, the female ferret will die of aplastic anaemia if she cannot find a mate.

- Reindeer eyes change from light brown to blue in winter.

- All snakes have vestigial legs from the time they ran around like other lizards. Now withered to tiny stumps, some species still use these to 'hold on' during mating.

- The *Turritopsis dohrnii* jellyfish reverts to infancy after mating. No one is sure how many times this cycle can be re-enacted but it is possible that the creature has achieved some sort of immortality.

- The duck-billed platypus lactates but has no nipples, nor does it have a stomach.

- Polar bears have black skin but their transparent fur scatters light to make them appear white.

- All spiders have forty-eight knees.

- The so-called killer whale is actually a dolphin; whales have no teeth! People just didn't like the sound of 'killer dolphin'.

DID YOU KNOW?

Sharks kill on average five people a year, cows kill about 100 and horses about 1,000.

THE MOST VENOMOUS ANIMALS ON THE PLANET

The box jellyfish – its venom is so powerful and fast-acting that victims have no chance of making it back to shore.

❖

The inland taipan snake of Australia delivers enough toxin in one bite to kill 100 adults.

❖

The king cobra, which injects five times the venom of the notorious black mamba.

❖

The marbled cone sea snail – one drop of its venom is enough to kill twenty adults.

❖

The stonefish – any who tread on them die instantly of shock.

❖

The blue-ringed octopus – one bite delivers enough venom to kill twenty-six adults in a minute.

❖

Poison dart frogs – one touch of their skin and you are toast.

❖

The pufferfish – on average, six deaths a year from poorly prepared *fugu*, as it is known in Japan.

DID YOU KNOW?

The term 'fish' is best left on the menu; in biological and evolutionary terms there is no such thing as a fish. In general terms, a 'fish' is any member of a paraphyletic group of organisms with a combination of gills and fins that lives in water.

10 OF THE MOST DEADLY

1. Humans have to take first place on this list, with about 750,000 detected homicides per year and over a million deaths on average as a result of war.

2. Next comes the mosquito, which by spreading malaria and other diseases kills about 1 million people every year.

3. Third are snakes which, between the species, kill about 50,000 people every year.

4. Fourth place goes to dogs, which kill about 25,000 people every year by rabies or by irreversible toxaemia from non-rabies bites that go bad. Very few people are actually savaged to death by dogs.

5. Fifth place goes to the assassin bug, which infects about a million South Americans every year with Chagas disease; the death toll is about 20,000 per year.

6. In sixth place we have a tie between the poisonous freshwater snail and the tsetse fly, which kill off roughly 10,000 people each per year.

7. Seventh place goes to the hippo, which – taking out over 3,000 people a year – is the most deadly quadruped in Africa.

8. Eighth place is taken by the African ascaris roundworm, an intestinal infestation caused by poor toilet hygiene that kills about 2,500 each year – so wash your hands!

9. In ninth place we have the humble tapeworm, which can migrate from the intestines to the brain to kill another 2,000 every year.

10. And tenth place goes to the crocodile, which kill just over 1,000 people annually.

ELEPHACTS

When a member of the herd dies, the rest gather round and stand guard – sometimes for days.

❖

An elephant can lift about 800 lb with its trunk.

❖

Albino elephants are in fact pink.

❖

Jumbo was the largest African elephant ever held in captivity, measuring 12 feet to the shoulder.

❖

About 500 people are killed every year by elephants, while people kill about 100,000 elephants in return.

❖

An elephant can detect the presence of water at distances of over 12 miles.

❖

Elephants spray themselves with dust to prevent sunburn.

❖

The average elephant weighs less than the tongue of the blue whale.

THE TRUTH ABOUT SHARKS

- While people kill over 100 million sharks every year, sharks themselves only kill about five people worldwide.

- Unlike scenes in *Jaws*, no shark actually swims along with a menacing dorsal fin showing above the surface. That fin is its main 'rudder' and will only appear if the creature strays into very shallow water.

- Although there are nearly 500 species of shark, only four are routinely involved in attacks on humans: the great white, the oceanic whitetip, the tiger and the bull.

- The largest shark is the 60-foot whale shark and the smallest is the 6-inch dwarf lantern shark.

- Although sharks are slaughtered in their millions to churn out anti-cancer shark-cartilage pills and other such hokum, sharks suffer from cancer themselves.

- Species such as the great white can detect blood in the water at dilutions of one drop in about 25 gallons but tales of them closing in from miles away are largely exaggerated.

That the shark has poor eyesight is a dangerous myth. Like the domestic cat, the shark has a tapetum, or mirror, at the back of the eye that fires the light back through the retina again, affording the creature a double take at everything it sees.

 Most sharks present eight rows of teeth so, if one on the outer line is lost, the tooth behind moves out to close the ranks like soldiers in battle.

 It is a myth that sharks must keep moving to stay alive. Some species take a 'nap' while pumping water across their gills with their mouths. Others 'park', nose up to a current and doze, holding themselves on station with gentle tail movements.

DID YOU KNOW?

With a diameter of over 10 inches, the eyes of the giant squid are the largest on the planet.

WILD CAT TALES

A lion's roar is audible at five miles.

❖

All the female lions of a pride are related.

❖

When a new male lion takes over he kills all the
cubs that are not of his line.

❖

There is no such animal as a panther – this is a lay
term used for black cougars, leopards and jaguars.

❖

A tiger can munch through about 25 kilos of meat
in one sitting.

❖

The leopard is the strongest of the big cats – it can
leap 6 metres and carry twice its own
body weight.

❖

The US has the largest population of tigers as more
live there in captivity than live wild throughout the
rest of the world.

DID YOU KNOW?

Elephants really do have good memories. Jenny, a resident of the Elephant Sanctuary in Hohenwald, Tennessee, was observed enacting the greeting ritual with newcomer Shirley in 1999. Background checks revealed both had been in the same circus for a few months – twenty-three years before.

WHO'S THE KING OF THE SWINGERS?

- Broadly speaking, the main difference between monkeys and apes is that the former have the tails and the latter have the brains.

- The gorilla was first seen in Sierra Leone in 480 BC by the Carthaginian Hanno the Navigator, who named them from the Greek *gorillai*, which means 'big hairy women'.

- Although human DNA only varies by 4 per cent from that of the chimpanzee, before anyone gets excited over that they should also consider that we have a 50 per cent similarity with the DNA of a banana.

- Even in a state of arousal, the gorilla's penis is just over an inch long; it is man who carries the largest penis of all the primates.

- Gorillas have been noted to casually rip the heads off those who annoy them, and one chimp on primatologist John Bauman's 1926 research programme pulled 1,260 lb on a dynamometer.

- In October 2012 a large troop of chimps inflicted a reprisal raid on the encroaching settlement of Tongo, in the Congo, killing ten people and leaving another seventeen with detached limbs.

DID YOU KNOW?

Birds do not sleep in their nests, which are built only for the young. The parents roost on nearby branches.

10 FACTS TO MAKE YOUR SKIN CRAWL

1. Medieval Taranto in Southern Italy was plagued by large wolf spiders whose bite was believed to be responsible for the recurrent bouts of dance mania in the city.

2. There are about 800 species of tarantula around the world but none is dangerous to man; a bite is both rare and non-fatal – a bit like a wasp sting.

3. The black widow was incorrectly named from the false belief that the female always eats the male after mating.

4. The bite of the Brazilian wandering spider induces priapism in male victims. Researchers are already hard at work to identify the constituent of the venom responsible for this natural alternative to Viagra.

5. There are about a million ants for every human on the planet.

6. Ninety per cent of all life on earth runs on six legs.

7. All insects carry their skeletons on the outside of their bodies.

8. A cockroach will live a month without its head as its breathing is not controlled by its brain but by spiracles in the body.

9. The smallest flying insect is the African parasitic wasp, which at 0.139 mm is smaller than the eye of a housefly.

10. With four noses, slugs are highly sensitive to gas, which is why they were used as an early warning system in First World War trenches.

QUIZ 1

A   What is the collective noun for rhinos?

B   Which animal lives in a sett?

C   Why can't owls move their eyes?

D   Male ducks, geese and swans are the only flying birds with what?

E   What colour is lobster blood?

F   Which is the only bird that can fly backwards but cannot walk?

G   What is the world's largest lizard?

H   What is the world's largest rodent?

I   What is the world's smallest mammal?

J   Which insect has no lungs and never sleeps?

K   How many stomachs does a cow have?

L   Most moths never eat. Why?

M   What colour is hippopotamus milk?

N   What kind of animal is a dik-dik?

O   Bats find their way about using radar – true or false?

ANSWERS TO QUIZ 1 NOT SO EASY — YOU'LL NEED A MIRROR TO CHECK THESE OUT!

A   A crash.

B   The badger.

C   Because their eyes are tubular in shape – the owl has to move its head to look around.

D   A penis.

E   Blue, as is the blood of snails and spiders.

F   The hummingbird.

G   The 12-foot Komodo dragon of Indonesia.

H   The South American capybara, which is basically a 100 lb hamster.

I   The bumblebee bat of Thailand. The Etruscan shrew is the next smallest.

J   The ant.

K   Four.

L   Few have stomachs and some don't even have mouths.

M   Pink.

N   A very small African deer – about 12 inches high.

O   False, they use sonar.

CELEBRITY AND INFAMY

FOR THE LOVE OF ART

Ernest Vincent Wright wrote the 50,000-word novel
Gadsby (1939) without a single 'e'.

✣

Van Gogh didn't cut off his ear; Gauguin cut it off
during one of their infamous brawls.

✣

Van Gogh didn't shoot himself; he was left-handed
and the bullet entered from the right. Prime suspect
is local thug Rene Secretan.

✣

Ian Fleming wrote all his books, including
Chitty-Chitty-Bang-Bang, at his Jamaican home
called Goldeneye.

The original Sherlock Holmes neither wore a deerstalker, nor said, 'Elementary, my dear Watson.'

❖

J. M. Barrie did not invent the name Wendy for *Peter Pan* – it appears in the census.

❖

The first book written on a typewriter was not Mark Twain's *Life on the Mississippi* (1883).

❖

While working on his books, Ernest Hemingway ate nothing but peanut butter sandwiches.

❖

Rejected by all mainstream publishers, Frank Herbert's *Dune* was eventually published by Chilton Books, best known for their car repair manuals.

❖

Swallows and Amazons author Arthur Ransome was a British spy in revolutionary Russia, implicated in an assassination attempt on Lenin.

❖

J. K. Rowling is the first person in history to achieve billionaire status through writing.

Toilet Trivia The most expensive loos are the gravity-lock ones used in the NASA space programme, which cost $19 million a piece.

FAMOUS DEATHS IN THE LOO

- Catherine the Great is said to have expired of sexual ecstasy while indulging in a very adult game of 'My Little Pony'. Not so; she collapsed after suffering a stroke in the loo and was carried to her bed where she died.

- Elvis Presley, obese and chronically constipated by the drugs he took, had a heart attack induced by his 'straining at stool'. He fell off the loo and died on the floor.

- In 1306, Wenceslaus III, teenaged king of Bohemia, Hungary and Poland, was sitting in his garderobe, a kind of enclosed loo that drained straight out to the moat, when some unkind soul shoved a spear up from below. A descendant of Good King Wenceslaus of Christmas-carol fame, he did not survive the experience.

It was said that Edmund Ironside (Edmund II) was likewise stabbed through the anus in 1016 by a Viking hiding in the void below the king's private garderobe.

British king George II was a slave to routine: last thing at night he always retired to the loo with a mug of hot chocolate. One night in 1760 he was found by his toilet attendant and pronounced dead from 'overexertion on the privy'.

UNSPORTING OLYMPIANS

ANCIENT CHEATS

Cheating in the ancient Olympics was widespread, with nation states often going to war over the results. Athletes breaking the rules were sometimes disqualified and subject to public whipping. When competitors and judges were found guilty of bribery, they were often faced with fines.

DRINK DRIVING

In the very first modern Olympics held in Athens in 1896, marathon runner Spyridon Belokas of Greece had to be disqualified from the race after it was revealed he had completed most of the course in a carriage, drinking wine and 'canoodling' with his girlfriend.

෩ඁ෨

FENCING FAKE

At the 1976 Montreal Olympics, Russian fencer Boris Onischenko scored countless hits on surprised opponents. It turned out that he had rigged his sword with a device that, at the touch of a button hidden in the handle, could register hits at will. Sent home in disgrace, he was packed off to the salt mines for a few years.

෩ඁ෨

A WELL-KEPT SECRET

Polish-American athlete Stella Walsh was the hottest sprinter of her day, winning countless medals, including gold and silver medals at the 1932 Los Angeles Olympics and the notorious 1936 meeting in Berlin. Shot by robbers of a convenience store in 1980, the autopsy revealed the secret of her success, with 'Stella's a Fella' a popular headline.

෩ඁ෨

HITCHING A RIDE

At the 1904 St Louis Olympics when it was revealed that New Yorker Fred Lorz had completed the last 11 miles in his trainer's car, the medal was passed to Thomas Hicks. Hicks turned out to be drugged up to the eyeballs, but he was allowed to keep the medal as there were no rules yet about doping.

❧❧❧

HITLER'S EMBARRASSMENT

Tipped for gold at the 1936 Berlin Games, Jewish high jumper Gretel Bergmann was bumped from the German team to save Hitler the embarrassment of congratulating her. So her roommate, Dora Ratjen, took her place to come fourth. At a 1938 German athletics event Dora was found to be male, with his genitals strapped back in a cache.

❧❧❧

FALL FROM GRACE

Ben Johnson won the 100 metres at the 1988 Seoul Olympics, but was later revealed to be a steroids cheat. Stripped of his medals and banned, he was hired in 1999 as fitness trainer to Saadi Gaddafi, son of the Libyan dictator. At his first outing in the Italian soccer league, Saadi also tested positive and, sent home in disgrace, he sacked Johnson.

❧❧❧

SEEING DOUBLE

Injured in the long jump at the 1984 Los Angeles Olympics, Madeline de Jesús of Puerto Rico was not up to running her qualifying heat for the 4 x 400 metres relay. Thinking she would be recovered for the main event, she got her twin sister, Margaret, to run the qualifier but the ruse was uncovered and both women banned.

✧

TUNISIAN FIASCO

At the 1960 Rome Games, the Tunisian pentathlon team all fell off their horses in the riding event, one nearly drowned in the swimming and they were all kicked out of the shooting event after one of them bounced a bullet off the forehead of an unimpressed judge. With only the fencing to go, they brought in a ringer thinking no one would check behind the mask – they were wrong.

✧

FAKE PARALYMPIANS

The organizers of the Spanish team attending the 2000 Paralympics at Sydney 'salted' their team with over fifteen perfectly healthy people who feigned physical or mental handicap to boost the medal tally. Those responsible were fined and the team were forced to return their medals.

✧

FANTASTIC FACTS ABOUT FASCISTS

Otherwise known as the Three-Week Führer, Admiral Karl Doenitz took over the running of Germany after Hitler's suicide on 30 April 1945. At the time, Doenitz was suffering from a urinary tract infection, resulting in severe incontinence and, upon his personal surrender to the Allies, he was found wearing six pairs of soggy underpants.

In November 1912 a scruffy little artist from Vienna went to visit his half-brother in Liverpool. Staying until the following April, Adolf Hitler was a regular in the local pubs and often seen supporting Everton on the terraces.

Benito Mussolini's youngest son, Romano, became a jazz pianist and, in 1961, married Anna Scicolone, Sophia Loren's sister.

Private Henry Tandey VC was fighting at the Battle of Cambrai in Northern France during the First World War when a wounded German stumbled out of the smoke. Tandey, unwilling to shoot an unarmed man, gestured the German to be gone. In 1937, that German wrote to Tandey's regimental HQ of the Green Howards requesting a portrait of the man who had spared him, signed Adolf Hitler.

FAMOUS PHOBICS

Oprah Winfrey is terrified of chewing gum and bans
it from her studios and offices.

❖

Pamela Anderson has a fear of mirrors.

❖

Nicole Kidman is scared of butterflies.

❖

Kelly Osbourne dreads being touched, especially
on her collarbone.

❖

An inveterate hypochondriac, Scarlett Johansson
has an irrational fear of birds.

❖

Megan Fox is phobic about loo paper and public
toilets; well, at least they go together.

❖

Madonna is scared witless by thunder.

❖

Jennifer Aniston, Whoopi Goldberg, and Cher are
all phobic about flying, as were Johnny Cash, Ray
Bradbury and President Reagan.

❖

Johnny Depp and Daniel Radcliffe are both
frightened by clowns.

❖

Orlando Bloom has a pig phobia while it is cows
that scare Lyle Lovett.

❖

Billy Bob Thornton can't breathe if there is antique
furniture in the room.

❖

Uma Thurman is claustrophobic, as indeed
was Hitler, President Reagan and, remarkably,
Harry Houdini.

❖

Baywatch star Carmen Electra is actually terrified
of the water.

❖

Kim Basinger and Daryl Hannah both have a dread
of open spaces, as did Marilyn Monroe.

❖

Sarah Michelle Gellar of Buffy fame has such a fear
of graveyards that she refuses to film in them.

❖

Hitler, Mussolini, Napoleon, Alexander the Great,
Julius Caesar and even Genghis Khan were all
terrified of cats.

❖

Keanu Reeves is frightened of the dark – as
was Gandhi.

❖

David Beckham suffers from OCD and
ataxophobia, the dread of disorder.

❖

Alfred Hitchcock was terrified by eggs and would
leave the table if anyone ordered an omelette.

❖

Woody Allen is phobic about heights, insects,
crowds, small rooms, bright colours, sunshine,
dogs, deer, elevators and children.

DID YOU KNOW?

From his confinement in Broadmoor asylum, demented murderer and self-castrator William Chester Minor was the
largest single compiling contributor to the first edition of
the *Oxford English Dictionary*.

INFAMOUS POLITICAL GAFFES

PUTIN'S KISS

During a walkabout in Moscow in 2006, Mr Putin drew a five-year-old-boy called Nikita from the crowd. He lifted his shirt and began kissing his stomach. His entourage was flabbergasted, as can be seen on internet footage of this odd event.

❧

MERKEL'S MASSAGE

At the G8 Summit in 2006, President George W. Bush suddenly stopped behind Angela Merkel's chair and began massaging her neck and shoulders. The horrified German Chancellor broke free with a two-armed manoeuvre she had learned at self-defence classes.

❧

CAMERON'S POPPY

British PM David Cameron caused great offence in China in the November of 2010 when he arrived sporting a Remembrance Day poppy. The Chinese still remember the Opium Wars the Victorians waged to force China to buy their Afghan-grown drugs.

❧

V IS FOR ... ?

As President Bush senior progressed through the streets of Canberra, Australia, in 1992, he amused the crowds by giving them the V-sign, wrongly thinking this the victory sign. Churchill often made the same mistake, as did Margaret Thatcher.

❧

A TRICKY HOUSE GUEST

On the first night of his 1995 White House visit, Boris Yeltsin was found in his underwear trying to hail a cab on Pennsylvania Avenue. He told the Secret Service agents he wanted a pizza. The next night he was nearly shot as an intruder as he drunkenly thrashed about in the basement of Blair House, the White House's guest residence.

❧

NOT A JOKING MATTER

Preparing for a national broadcast in 1984, Reagan, unaware his mic was live, joked, 'My fellow Americans, I am pleased to tell you today that I've signed legislation that will outlaw Russia for ever. We begin bombing in five minutes.' The Kremlin was furious.

❧

DID YOU KNOW?

The 1912 Olympics in Stockholm saw the last gold medals actually made from gold – from then on they were gold-plated.

ONE DOESN'T HUG

During a State visit to the UK, Michelle Obama caused gasps of horror when she breached protocol by greeting the Queen with an enthusiastic embrace.

✦

PRINCE PHILIP

Already famous for greeting the Nigerian president in national costume by asking if he was ready for bed, Prince Philip famously once greeted traditionally adorned Aboriginal leaders in Australia by asking if they still chucked spears at each other.

✦

LOST IN TRANSLATION

President Carter's 1977 visit to Poland was enlivened by the shortcomings of his translator, Steven Seymour. When Carter proclaimed he was there to learn the Poles' hopes for the future, Seymour informed the assembly that Carter 'had carnal desires for all Poles'.

✦

BERLUSCONI'S BLOOPER

Welcoming the Obamas at the opening of their 2008 visit to Rome, Silvio Berlusconi caused assembled jaws to drop by complimenting the pair on their suntans.

~~~

THE NOT-SO-ETERNAL FLAME

During an understandably sensitive visit to Israel's Yad Vashem Holocaust Memorial in 2000, German Chancellor Gerhard Schroeder absent-mindedly fiddled with a switch and turned off the Eternal Flame in the centrepiece.

~~~

BUSH'S BANQUET BLUNDER

At the official banquet to welcome President Bush senior to Japan in 1992, the food obviously did not agree with the visitor who turned and vomited into the lap of the Japanese prime minister. Having finished, Bush fainted and slipped under the table.

~~~

DON'T SHOOT THE HOST

Invited in 2006 to a quail hunt at the home of Texas Attorney Harry Whittington, Vice President Dick Cheney managed to shoot his host with a shotgun. With over thirty pellets in his face, neck and torso, Whittington ended up in intensive care.

NOT READY FOR HIS CLOSE-UP

In 1993, British Secretary of State for Wales John Redwood dutifully rose to his feet at the Welsh Conference during the opening bars of the Welsh anthem. The cameras closed in on his face as all realized he had not bothered to learn the words and was miming worse than any pop star.

DID YOU KNOW?

Both golf and football were banned in 1457 by James II who was concerned that men were being distracted from the more valuable practice of archery.

DID YOU KNOW?

Only since January 2013 has it been legal for women to wear trousers in Paris. The 1799 ban was rigorously enforced, with Marlene Dietrich and Katharine Hepburn both run out of the city in 1938 for wearing slacks.

13 SPORTING HEROES-TURNED-POLITICIAN

1. WWE wrestling star Jesse Ventura quit the ring for politics when he became Governor of Minnesota in 1999.

2. British tennis star Buster Mottram got involved in extreme right-wing politics and was expelled from UKIP in 2008 for trying to broker an election pact between UKIP and the British National Party.

3. Big Arnie Schwarzenegger was once a professional bodybuilder and holder of the Mr Universe and Mr Olympia titles before he quit Hollywood to become the Governor of California in 2003.

4. Colin Moynihan, who sat in the Thatcher cabinet, was previously a rowing ace, winning gold and silver medals in the World Rowing Championships and the Olympic games.

5. Cricketing star Ted Dexter stood for parliament in the Cardiff South East district in 1964 only to lose out to James 'Sunny Jim' Callaghan.

6. Before he was a rising star in Thatcher's government, Jeffrey Archer was an athlete who raced for both England and Britain.

7. Olympic distance runner Christopher Chataway quit the track for politics in 1958 when to took the seat for Lewisham North for the Conservatives.

8. In the 1960s, Menzies Campbell, Leader of the Liberal Democrats from 2006–7, was known in his sporting days as 'the fastest white man on the planet', once running the 100 metres in 10.2 seconds, beating O. J. Simpson into second place.

9. Sebastian Coe was a middle-distance Olympic legend before he became MP for Falmouth and Camborne in 1992. As a life peer, he now sits in the House of Lords.

10. Footballer George Weah, who had played for Paris Saint-Germain, AC Milan and Chelsea, went home to Liberia in 2005 to win the first round of the presidential elections. He was later elected to the Liberian Senate in 2014.

11. Pakistani cricketing star Imran Khan founded his own party in 1996 and has since been a major political player in Pakistan.

12. Russian chess champion Garry Kasparov founded his United Civil Front in 2005 to present a seriously vocal opposition to Vladimir Putin.

13. Before he went home to Cuba in 1959 to start his takeover bid, Fidel Castro was a Minor League Baseball player in the US. There are persistent but unsubstantiated rumours that he tried out for the New York Yankees.

SILLY NAMES IN SPORT

Jordin Tootoo – Canadian ice hockey star.

❖

Gaylord Silly – Seychelles distance runner.

❖

Irinia Slutskaya – Russian ice dancer.

❖

Jean Condom – French rugby international.

❖

Dick Sisler – American Major League Baseball star.

❖

Yoshi Takeshita – Japanese volleyball star.

❖

Dick Felt – American football star.

❖

Destinee Hooker – female American volleyball star.

❖

Misty Hyman – American women's swimming
medallist.

❖

Ricky van Wolfswinkle – Lisbon soccer star.

QUIZ 2

A   What was Jerome K. Jerome's middle name?

B   Who was assassinated in Memphis, Tennessee, in 1968?

C   What film was showing in the *Titanic*'s cinema the night she sank?

D   For which crime did Shakespeare do time?

E   What did DNA testing of the body tissue found in Dr Crippen's cellar recently reveal?

F   Why was American tennis star Renée Richards banned from the 1976 Wimbledon women's singles?

G   Which American tycoon kept a signed photo of Hitler on his desk throughout the Second World War?

H   Where was actor Mel Gibson born?

I   Churchill confessed to a gay relationship with which famous singer?

J   Who was the first American saint?

K   Can you name the only English pope?

L   Which fashion designer made the black SS uniforms?

M   Which role has been played by Donald Pleasence, Telly Savalas and Charles Gray?

N   Retired to Los Angeles, Wyatt Earp befriended which future cowboy star?

ANSWERS TO QUIZ 2 NOT SO EASY — YOU'LL NEED A MIRROR TO CHECK THESE OUT!

A Klapka.

B Martin Luther King.

C The Poseidon Adventure (1911) by D. W. Griffiths.

D Poaching.

E That the victim had been male and thus not Crippen's wife.

F Because she was a transgender man.

G Henry Ford.

H New York – his family moved to Australia when he was twelve.

I Ivor Novello; Churchill spoke of it to Somerset Maugham.

J Elizabeth Seton (1774-1821), founder of the Sisters of Charity.

K Nicholas Breakspear (1100-59) aka Pope Adrian IV.

L Hugo Boss.

M Blofeld, the villain of the Bond movies.

N John Wayne, who said he modelled his on-screen persona on Earp.

DISCOVER THIS! CHANGING THE WORLD ONE INVENTION AT A TIME

INCREDIBLY STUPID WEAPONS

OPERATION ACOUSTIC KITTY

In 1961 the CIA decided to surgically implant cats with bugging devices and aerials in their tails. The idea was to get the cats into Soviet enclaves, especially the Kremlin, with the first feline agent released outside the Soviet compound in Washington where it was instantly turned into $15 million worth of roadkill by a speeding motorist. Operation Acoustic Kitty was finally shut down in 1967.

༺ ❦ ༻

THE BAT BOMB

After spending millions on Operation Dracula, the Americans abandoned the bat bomb in 1944. The idea was to attach small incendiary bombs to the bats before dropping them in their thousands over Japanese cities. And it worked, sort of: in their first test deployment the bats' homing instinct brought them back to the project base at Carlsbad Airbase in New Mexico, which they successfully burned to the ground.

❧

ANTI-TANK DOG

Inspired by the work of Pavlov, the Russian army invented the anti-tank dog. The dogs were starved for days on end and then let out to gorge on food laid out under tanks. The idea was to starve the dogs before a battle, strap mines to their backs and turn them loose. But, conditioned to the smell of diesel from the Russian tanks they were trained on – the German Panzers ran on petrol – on their first outing the dogs forced three brigades of Russian armour into a panicked retreat.

❧

DID YOU KNOW?

Hairdryers did not really take off until the 1960s. Before that women often locked the hoover hose into the hot exhaust outlet and used that.

HIMMLER'S SEX DOLLS

Alarmed at the number of troops infected with syphilis, Himmler instituted the Borghild Project to produce silicone sex dolls to keep Hitler's troops out of the brothels. The prototypes, made by Dr Olen Hannussen of Berlin's SS Hygiene Institute, were sent for field trials at the German barracks on Jersey. Clearly the trials were not a success as the project was scrapped.

৩৯৬৯

RUSSIAN ROULETTE

Back in the 1870s the Russians came up with the idea of circular battleships and launched the *Popov* and the *Novgorod*. Both were heavily armed but each time anyone fired any of the guns placed about the circumference, the ships spun wildly, throwing the gun crews overboard. Amusing though it sounds, this novel form of Russian roulette was soon abandoned.

৩৯৬৯

THE GAY BOMB

In 1994 the USAF Research Laboratory at Wright-Patterson airbase in Ohio was working on not only the flatulence bomb but also the gay bomb. The idea of the gay bomb was to disperse pheromones designed to make enemy soldiers forget all about fighting, having suddenly found each other sexually irresistible.

৩৯৬৯

SERENDIPITY...

Invention usually comes about through years of hard work and endless trials. Yet here are some brought into being by accident or genuine error.

- In 1987 Dr Jean Carruthers of Vancouver was treating a patient with injections of deadly botulism to cure her facial spasms. Carruthers noticed a cosmetic enhancement and so Botox was born.

- Returning from an Alpine hunting trip in 1941, Swiss electrical engineer George de Mestral was infuriated by the number of burdock burrs attached to his clothing and to the fur of his beloved dog. Examination under a microscope revealed the spikes on the burrs to have hooked ends and de Mestral went on to make a fortune out of the Velcro inspired by that simple observation.

- In 1946 Swiss chemist Albert Hofmann was researching the ergot fungus that attacked rye crops. Having reduced it to a tartrate to make it easier to study, Hofmann inadvertently ingested some micro-fine particles in his lab. After a six-hour technicolour bike ride around Basel, he realized he had invented LSD.

Tinkering in his lab at Cornell University in 1958, Wilson Greatbatch installed the wrong transistor into a device linked to an oscilloscope and heard a noise remarkably similar to the human heartbeat. This mistake lead to the first generation of pacemakers.

In 1880 Herman Hollerith sat watching a train conductor, intrigued that he punched passengers' tickets in different places. The conductor explained that he did this to prevent two or more people riding on the same ticket, e.g. the placement of the hole indicated gender, age and so on. The IBM punch card system came soon after.

In 1867 Alfred Nobel accidentally damaged a container of nitroglycerine, which leaked its contents into the cheap kieselguhr used to buffer the jars. Happily absorbing the explosive, the clay turned into a putty that could be modelled into sticks. Nobel patented this new form as dynamite.

DID YOU KNOW?

The wheelbarrow was invented in early China, not for gardening, but as a means for the army to transport war materials along the narrow dams between the paddy fields.

🧻 After a hard day in 1879 trying to synthesize benzoic sulfimide at Johns Hopkins University, Constantin Fahlberg couldn't be bothered to wash his hands before going home. Noticing the sweet taste on his hands as he ate dinner, he rushed back to the lab to find his failed attempts at synthesis had produced what he would later register as Saccharin.

🧻 In 1945 Percy Spencer was demonstrating a new radar to USAF officers when he became aware of an embarrassing brown stain spreading across his clothing. Backing sheepishly out of the room to the corridor, he realized that a forgotten chocolate bar had been melted by the radar's magnetron. He would use this new science to create the microwave oven.

🧻 In the late 1980s, drug company Pfizer felt it was time to test its new angina drug UK-92480 on human subjects in clinical trials. All of the male participants in those trials reported that something else had begun to function again! The company forgot about angina and marketed the drug as Viagra.

THE TRUE HISTORY OF THE FLUSHING LOO

VINEGAR AND A SPONGE

Back in ancient Rome they built communal loos comprising a long bench with about thirty holes cut into it and no partitions. Having no loo paper, Romans cleaned up with a sponge dipped in vinegar that was then passed down the line.

❧

STOOL BOYS

Those caught short in seventeenth-century London would whistle up the nearest stool boy. He would arrive equipped with a bucket and cloak to shroud his customers while they relieved themselves right there in the street.

❧

DID YOU KNOW?

Lonnie Johnson was the man who developed stealth bomber technology; in a more frivolous moment, he also invented the Super Soaker water gun.

Toilet Trivia

To allow for segregation, the Pentagon was built with nearly 300 toilets instead of the 150 it needed. Today it gets through 700 loo rolls a day.

THE BOURDALOUE

European ladies of the seventeenth century always carried their bourdaloue on coach trips, or when out at social events. Carefully crafted for them to pee in without spillage, they would be handed to a maid to empty out. At modern auctions many of these are sold to people who mistake them for gravy boats!

GEORGE JENNINGS

Although there had been crude flushing loos around since the sixteenth century, sanitary engineer George Jennings developed the first workable version. He was contracted to install it in the 'Retiring Rooms' of Crystal Palace's 1851 Great Exhibition.

THE FIRST PUBLIC LOO

Sir Samuel Morton Peto and Sir Henry Cole built London's first public loos. The coin-operated cubicle doors took a penny – hence 'spending a penny'. Interestingly, Peto also built Nelson's Column and Cole was the inventor of the Christmas card.

CRAPPER

Next to throw his hat into the ring was the appositely named Thomas Crapper who, in the late 1880s, patented his symphonic flushing system, still used today. Although touted as the origin of the vulgar 'crap', that term had been used for years before Crapper was even born.

తౖౖౖ

RECENT INNOVATIONS

In 1993 a company came up with the Urinelle, commonly known as the shewee. This cleverly shaped funnel allows women to wee standing, avoiding contact with the loo. The Japanese have recently developed a musical loo that, connected to the internet, will email your doctor if it detects blood or raised sugar levels. It automatically warms its own seat at times of regular use or you can ring it up to let it know you will be home soon. It is also voice-activated and will talk back to you.

తౖౖౖ

DID YOU KNOW?

The Swiss didn't invent the cuckoo clock. These first appeared in the Black Forest during the seventeenth century. The Swiss later stole the design to sell clocks to tourists.

INVENTIONS NAMED AFTER PEOPLE

Bakelite – Leo Baekeland, Belgian-born chemist.

❖

Belisha Beacon – Leslie Hore-Belisha, Minister of
Transport in the 1930s.

❖

Biro – Lázló Bíró, inventor.

❖

Bloomers – Amelia Jenks Bloomer, women's rights
advocate.

❖

Braille – Louis Braille, French educator and inventor.

❖

Callanetics – Callan Pinckney, fitness professional.

❖

Cardigan – James Brudenell, 7th Earl of Cardigan,
who led the Charge of the Light Brigade.

❖

Catherine Wheel – St Catherine of Alexandria,
martyred on a burning wheel.

❖

LEARN ON THE LOO

Ferris Wheel – George Ferris Jr., American engineer.

❖

Gallup poll – George Gallup, polling-company
owner and pioneer.

❖

Guillotine – Joseph-Ignace Guillotin, French
physician and freemason.

❖

Peach Melba – Dame Nellie Melba, Australian
operatic soprano.

❖

Pavlova – Anna Pavlova, Russian prima ballerina.

❖

Leotard – Jules Léotard, French trapeze artist.

❖

Sandwich – John Montagu, 4th Earl of Sandwich.

❖

Saxophone – Antoine-Joseph 'Adolphe' Sax,
Belgian musician and designer.

INVENTIONS FOR THE FUTURE

BACK TO THE FUTURE

Researchers in France have already managed to create a self-levitating skateboard as seen in the Back to the Future films and are now trying to extend this technology to a road-going vehicle.

∽◦⊙◦∾

TIDAL POWER

The company of Blue Energy Canada has developed subway-sized underwater turbines to harness tidal power; they have already signed contracts with India and New Zealand where they hope to have oceanic hydro-electrical programmes up and running in the next ten years.

∽◦⊙◦∾

THE HEALTH CHIP

Intelligent nano implants to monitor your body's health are not that far away. A research programme in the Netherlands has developed a pill that can be loaded with medicine and then programmed to travel to a specific location in the body and discharge its tiny cargo.

∽◦⊙◦∾

'PRINTING' BODY PARTS

3D printing has been around for a while now but pharmaceutical companies are trying to develop ways to use it to 'print' human tissue for reconstructive purposes and organ replacement.

꿍

PROSTHETICS

DEKA Research has already developed a prosthetic forearm that can pick up electrical impulses from the stump to which it is attached and perform many functions; they are now working on other prosthetics that take their signals directly from the brain.

꿍

EXOSKELETONS

Superhero-style exoskeletons are in development at the University of Pennsylvania's Titan Arm project. These will allow ordinary wearers to achieve superhuman strength and the paralysed to become mobile again.

꿍

THE 600-MPH TRAIN

Tesla and SpaceX are two companies working to make high-speed, low-friction trains a reality. They already have a 600 mph working model they reckon could carry passengers from LA to San Francisco in thirty minutes.

꿍

THE ONE THAT GOT AWAY

In 1993 an episode of the television programme *Tomorrow's World* opened up with an egg held in a clamp under the direct blast of a blowtorch. After five minutes the egg was not only cold, but still raw. It had been coated in Starlite, as developed by Yorkshire hairdresser Maurice Ward. In further tests, the US Atomic Test Centre hit Starlite with blasts of energy equivalent to seventy-five Hiroshimas and only managed to blacken the sample in one small spot. Unfortunately Ward died before he could tell anyone what Starlite was.

3 DISASTROUS EXPEDITIONS

1. The nineteen-man trans-Australian Burke and Wills expedition of 1860 set out from Melbourne amid much fanfare. Grossly overladen, however, they only made four miles on the first day and had to make camp within sight of their own homes. They made it to the Gulf of Carpentaria in the north and halfway back to Cooper's Creek where, with all supplies exhausted, the racist Burke opened fire on approaching natives who had come bearing food and water to save the strangers in their midst. The locals sensibly scattered and left the party to die.

2. Believing H. Rider Haggard's eternally youthful *She* to be rooted in reality, English explorer Percy Fawcett set out for the Brazilian jungle in 1925 to find the mythical city of Z, as he called it. Hopelessly ill-equipped for a trek in such terrain, he was never seen again. Of the fifteen subsequent expeditions that set off to find out what happened, over a hundred people died trying to retrace his steps.

3. In November 1873 Alfred Packer led a party of twenty-one gold prospectors out of Provo in Utah bound for the Rockies. Ignoring warnings of heavy snow, they got lost in the mountains. Packer was quick to realize that the only fresh meat he would see before the thaw was stamping about the camp bemoaning his ineptitude. Although he claimed self-defence, he was eventually tried and sentenced.

DID YOU KNOW?

In the 1930s, Ford offered a barbecue frame to fit over its car engines so you could cook your meat en route to your picnic site.

INVENTIONS NAMED AFTER PLACES

Angostura Bitters – Angostura, the old name for
Ciudad Bolivar in Venezuela.

❧

Balaclava – the Battle of Balaklava in the
Crimean War.

❧

Bikini – Bikini Atoll in the Marshall Islands, site of
first peacetime nuclear test.

❧

Denim – Nîmes in France (de Nîmes).

❧

Dumdum bullet – Dum Dum, an arsenal and town
outside Kolkata.

❧

Fez – the town of Fez in Morocco.

❧

Jeans – Genoa in Italy.

❧

Limousine – Limousin in France.

❧

Mayonnaise – Mahón in Menorca.

QUIZ 3

A   Where in the world was the yo-yo invented?

B   Which Persian invention was brought to the UK by the
Romans and adopted by the Scots?

C   Which celebrated British scientist invented the cat flap?

D   Which popular drink was invented by John Pemberton and
first sold as Pemberton's Brain Tonic?

E   What did the Roman Emperor Elagabalus invent to
embarrass his dinner guests as they sat down?

F   What did Richard Gatling invent in 1861?

G   What were the first ever words recorded on the Edison
phonograph?

H   What did Mary Phelps Jacob invent in 1914?

I   Why was the parachute invented before aircrafts were even
thought of?

J   What product did 3M launch after it realized its new glue
would not set properly?

K   Which British monarch wrote 'Greensleeves'?

L   William Marston, creator of *Wonder Woman*, invented
which interrogation device?

M   In 1904 Elizabeth Magie invented a board game to teach
economic theory; what is it called today?

N   Bette Nesmith Graham, mother of Mike Nesmith of *The
Monkees*, invented which stationery item?

ANSWERS TO QUIZ 3
NOT SO EASY — YOU'LL NEED A MIRROR TO CHECK THESE OUT!

A   In the Philippines, where hunters hiding in trees could hit small game on the ground below.

B   The bagpipe, always singular as there are many drones but only one pipe or chanter.

C   Isaac Newton.

D   Coca-Cola.

E   The whoopee cushion.

F   The first machine gun.

G   'Mary had a little lamb', as recorded in 1927 by Edison himself.

H   The modern bra.

I   For people in hot-air balloons.

J   Post-it notes.

K   Henry VIII designed it to get him up and down stairs at Whitehall Palace.

L   The lie detector.

M   Monopoly. She sold the game for $250 so she was the one in need of a lesson in economics.

N   Liquid Paper (correction fluid) to correct typos – but she sold out for $48 million.

AROUND THE WORLD: COUNTRY TO COUNTRY

13 THINGS YOU DIDN'T KNOW ABOUT CHINA AND JAPAN

1. The geisha, or art-people, were originally all male; not until the nineteenth century did the women really take over. There are still male geisha, normally referred to as *taikomochi*.

2. The black-clad ninja is a Western invention. Ninjas were mainly spies, female domestic staff and such. Samurai were hired for assassinations.

3. Numerological superstition is very strong in China where no building has a thirteenth floor.

4. Japanese educationalist Elizabeth Lee visited England and was so taken with the Royal Navy uniform that she introduced it to Japanese girls' academies of the 1920s. Known in Japan as the *fuku*, this is still standard schoolgirl attire.

5. Home to one of the world's most non-PC theme parks, China is under pressure to close its Kingdom of the Little People, just outside Kunming, where hordes of dwarves entertain the visitors.

6. In China, darker skin is still the stigma of the lower orders so ski masks are standard beachwear for the rich and pampered.

7. Chinese and Japanese write top to bottom and right to left because they first wrote on bamboo. Held and turned by the left hand, this was the only way to prevent smudging previous characters.

8. The Japanese yakuza (organized crime) takes its name from the losing hand in the card game of *Hanafuda*, or 'flower cards'. *Ya*, *ku* and *za* is Japanese for 8, 9 and 3, the lowest possible hand.

9. In Mandarin, *shi* has so many meanings that there is a famous poem that repeats the term ninety-two times – and still makes sense.

10. Numbering in excess of 54 million, China has more Christians than any other nation.

11. Getting through over 80 billion pairs of chopsticks each year, China is now under pressure to use cutlery to save resources.

12. Having adopted some of the more calorific aspects of the Western diet, average height in China has increased by 6 centimetres in the past twenty years.

13. Despite its teeming millions, China has only 1,000 regularly used surnames from a total of about 4,000.

Toilet Trivia Toilet paper was invented in China in the fourteenth century but was reserved for Imperial use only.

WHAT'S IN A NAME?

Nearly everyone on earth knows about Apple and Adidas, but from which countries do these international brands originate and what's the history behind them? Here are a few you might have heard of.

CITROËN

From a family of Dutch lemonade makers, by 1904 André Citroën was making helical gearwheels with interlocking chevron teeth. His first major contract was to supply the steering system for RMS *Titanic* but, for some reason, Citroën has never bothered to advertise that fact. Either way, such beginnings explain the present company logo.

◈

APPLE

The co-founder of American company Apple, Ronald Wayne came up with the company logo from the myth of Isaac Newton being hit on the head by an apple and the reality of the Father of Computing, Alan Turing, committing suicide with a cyanide-laced apple after being 'outed' (hence the missing bit of the apple).

DID YOU KNOW?

Both ketchup and football seem to have developed in China sometime in the second or third century BC.

MARMITE

This is the old French word for a hypocrite, which also became the nickname of the kind of heavy-lidded cooking pot featured on the Marmite label. Invented by a German, Justus von Liebig, Marmite was then manufactured in Britain. Marmite is in fact the brand name for two similar spreads – the original British version, and one produced in New Zealand. British Marmite was first served in large earthenware pots, with the glass jar we're familiar with now coming in during the 1920s.

୧୭୭୭

NINTENDO

Founded in Kyoto in 1889 by Fusajiro Yamauchi, Nintendo is thought to mean 'entrust your luck to heaven', and the company started off by producing handmade *Hanafuda* playing cards. It is now the largest video-games company in the world.

୧୭୭୭

GREYHOUND BUS COMPANY

Crippled by an accident at 3M's mining facility in Minnesota, Carl Wickman bought some eight-seater Hupmobiles to run miners to and from the site. Like everything else in the area, his vehicles were coated in grey dust from the mine and, because they moved the passengers swiftly to their destination, they were nicknamed the greyhounds.

୧୭୭୭

ADIDAS AND PUMA

German designers and brothers Adolf and Rudolf Dassler fell out over which had been the more ardent Nazi during the war. Going their separate ways, Adolf founded sports brand Adidas from 'Dassler' and 'Adi', while Rudolf founded Ruda which, frequently misheard as Puma, took that name in 1948. The two companies were still feuding until 2009.

～～～

SCOTCH TAPE

The 1920s American trend for two-tone cars prompted 3M to test-market a 2-inch masking tape for spray shops, but they skimped on the adhesive and the tape kept falling off. Inspired by the groundless myth of Scottish parsimony, the sprayers nicknamed it Scotch tape and the name stuck.

～～～

MERCEDES

In 1899 the Austrian Emil Jellinek, the biggest dealer in Daimler cars in Europe, entered the Tour de Nice under the pseudonym of Mercedes, the name of his ten-year-old daughter. Winning the race, he kept the name for his company as it expanded across Europe and the US.

DID YOU KNOW?

Straddling the divide between Europe and Asia, Istanbul is the only major city to stand in two continents.

VASELINE

The year 1859 saw American chemist Robert Chesebrough working in the Pennsylvania oil fields where he noticed the riggers would treat minor cuts and injuries with a gunk that came up on the drilling rods. This he refined and marketed, mercifully abandoning his initial name of Rod Oil in favour of Vaseline Petroleum Jelly, as inspired by the German for water and the Greek for oil.

∽◎◎◎◇

BIRDSEYE

In 1915 American inventor and entrepreneur Clarence Birdseye was injured in Labrador, in northerly Newfoundland, and taken in by the Inuit. He watched them dipping food in water and exposing it to the elements and realized that the speed of the freeze ensured the meat did not thaw out as mush. Once recovered, he established his now-famous company in New York.

∽◎◎◎◇

4711 COLOGNE

In 1794 the French took Cologne and, finding the maze of streets a nightmare, they divided the city into sectors and numbered every street and house. The small perfume factory at 13 Bell Lane became house 11 in Street 7 of Sector 4. The tiny bell on the label is a nod to the original address.

∽◎◎◎◇

JAGUAR

Starting out in the 1920s as the Swallow Sidecar Company, the British organization moved from motorbikes to cars in the 1930s, calling themselves the SS Car Company. The Second World War rendered this name a no-no, so Jaguar was picked at random with a pin from a list of swift animals.

⟡⟡⟡⟡

SHELL

In 1833 Marcus Samuel took his family to the British seaside to gather seashells to decorate boxes, which he then sold in his London venture, The Shell Shop. Turning to the East for more exotic shells, he also got involved in the importation of oils and the rest, as they say…

⟡⟡⟡⟡

AUDI

In the early 1900s German engineer August Horch was fiddled out of his car company and banned from using his own name when he set up in competition. As his name meant 'hear' or 'listen' in German, he opted for the Latin equivalent – Audi!

⟡⟡⟡⟡

A VERY POPULATED PLANET

Instituted in 1979, China's one-child policy has so far resulted in the infanticide of over 100 million girls, as sons are more favoured. Already there are about 30 million Chinese men with no hope of finding a wife.

Buenos Aires has the highest ratio of psychoanalysts per capita of any city. Argentina itself has 202 shrinks per 100,000 members of the population, with Austria coming a poor second with only 80 per 100,000.

Only 1 per cent of the islands in the Caribbean are populated and Cuba is the only one with a railway.

The Polish population of Chicago is second in number only to that of Warsaw.

The original Japanese were the Ainu, a tall Eurasian-like people, many of whom had blue eyes. Largely driven out about 10,000 years ago, only 25,000 remain in Japan today (they were replaced by Chinese, Korean and Polynesian invaders).

- With a population of about 37,500 packed into its 1 square mile, Monaco is the most densely populated country on the planet.

- Mongolia, with a population of about 3,200,000 scattered across its 603,909 sq mi, is the least densely populated.

- Over 30 million Chinese in the rural north still live in caves called *yaodongs*.

- Canada is the country with the most lakes and over 85 per cent of the population live within 100 miles of the US border.

- A percentage of Moscow's feral dogs live in the underground system and attracted international attention after it was realized they had learned which trains to take to travel the city, visiting their favourite parks and foraging sites.

Toilet Trivia

Most conventional toilets flush in the key of E flat.

FLAGS OF THE WORLD

Believe it or not, the famous Nazi salute was inspired by the Americans, who pledged allegiance to their flag with a right-armed salute.

❖

The study of flags is called vexillology, after the Vexillium of the Roman army, who was burdened with the duty of carrying the banner.

❖

Having published his philosophical musings in his 'Green Book', Libyan leader Colonel Gaddafi decreed the national flag be a plain green rectangle with no features.

❖

National flags tend to be rectangular and battle flags square but the Vatican and perennially neutral Switzerland have square flags.

❖

Hawaii is the only American state to have a Union Jack on its flag.

❖

The only national flag showing a modern weapon is that of Mozambique, which features an AK-47 with a fixed bayonet.

❖

Nepal has the only national flag that is neither square nor rectangular – it's two conjoined red pennants with blue borders.

❖

No real pirate ever flew the skull and cross bones. Most flew nothing at all until they closed in on a victim and then raised a plain black flag, which was the signal to surrender.

❖

Adopted around 1370, the Danish flag presenting a white cross on a red background is the oldest national flag still flying.

❖

The Royal Standard of Britain is the only flag that is never half-masted, as the instant a monarch dies they are replaced by a successor.

Toilet Trivia

Bidet is the French for a pony so small that the rider has to lift their feet off the ground to ride it.

WORLD AT WAR

BATTEN DOWN THE HATCHES

Fearing invasion during the Second World War, the Swiss mined every tunnel, bridge and rail-link into the country. Today the Swiss can still isolate themselves at the flick of a switch.

❧

BATTLE ON ICE

The only naval battle won by cavalry was fought on the Sea of Texel in the Netherlands on 20 January 1795. A Dutch fleet, come to attack the French, had anchored up and awoke to find themselves ice-bound. The French cavalry fitted spiked horse shoes to their horses and charged across the ice to capture all fourteen ships without a shot being fired.

❧

SPOILS OF WAR

The tall bearskin hats worn by the British Guards were first pinched from captured French guardsmen after Waterloo and taken home as trophies. The other harvest was the teeth torn out of the fallen and sold to dentists to make dentures, later known as Waterloo Teeth.

❧

WHO'S FIGHTING WHO?

Although seen as a Scotland vs England affair, at the Battle of Culloden (1746) there were more Scottish fighting on the English side than were in the entire Scottish Army.

⋅⊙⊙⊙⋅

AEROBATICS

The only fighter pilot to fall out of his plane and get back in was the nobly named Sir Grahame Donald. Testing out his new Sopwith Camel in 1917, he went for a loop at 6,000 feet and fell out of the plane. Fortunately for him, the Camel continued its loop with Donald landing on the wing as it passed under him.

⋅⊙⊙⊙⋅

AN INSTANT ARMY

Every able-bodied Swiss male undergoes military training and is obliged to keep an assault rifle and a stash of ammunition at home. If the call is raised, Switzerland could field an instant army of over 500,000.

⋅⊙⊙⊙⋅

DID YOU KNOW?

In Hawaii, if a woman is wearing a flower over her left ear it means that she is not open to approaches.

A STRATEGIC MOVE

The only military campaign settled by a game of chess was that waged by King Alfonso VI of León and Castile in 1078. Alfonso had besieged the Moors in Seville but all was at deadlock so, knowing Alfonso to be a chess nut, the Moors suggested he play their champion, Ben Ammar, to decide the matter. Alfonso lost the game and, true to his word, withdrew his forces.

৵৩৩৩৩

STILL AT WAR

Japan and Russia are still officially at war with neither nation signing the peace treaties after the Second World War due to an on-going dispute over the Kuril Islands.

৵৩৩৩৩

PLAN RED

There were red faces in the White House in 1974 when details of Plan Red were revealed. A blueprint for attacking the UK, it included pre-emptive strikes on Canada and Australia.

৵৩৩৩৩

NOT A MOMENT'S PEACE

Peace on earth and goodwill to all men? Throughout the past 3,000 years not a day has passed when there hasn't been a war going on somewhere in the world.

৵৩৩৩৩

VICTORIA CROSS

Popularly believed to be made from the pommels of Russian guns captured in the Crimean War, the first Victoria Crosses were in fact made from Chinese cannon captured in the First Opium War.

OOPS!

The 'neutral' Swiss did so much business with Nazi Germany that there were about forty 'Oops, *quel dommage*!' bombing raids on major Swiss cities. After each such 'reminder' the Allies claimed faulty navigation.

SWISS ACTION

Having had so few wars of their own – fewer than twenty since the fourteenth century – Swiss men were hired out as mercenaries to get a bit of action. They fought in everything from the French Revolution (on the losing side) to the Zulu Wars (on the winning side). Since 1859, only the mercenaries guarding the Vatican are sanctioned under Swiss law.

DID YOU KNOW?

Whenever a pope dies he is hit on the head three times with a special silver hammer, just to make sure.

BIZARRE RITUALS, FESTIVALS AND CULTS FROM AROUND THE WORLD

THE FESTIVAL OF THE HOLY PREPUCE

Every year, from 1557 to 1983, the Italian town of Calcata paraded their prized relic in the Festival of the Holy Prepuce. For years the Vatican had tried in vain to dissuade the townsfolk from displaying what they claimed to be Jesus's circumcised foreskin but even threats of excommunication failed to do the trick. It is rumoured that in 1983 some Dan Brown-style cleric was dispatched from Rome to steal the relic and thus put an end to the matter.

ఆర్(రా)ఎం

AN UNPLEASANT DIET

Hinduism decrees that holy men, children, pregnant or unmarried women and those who have died from snake bite or leprosy cannot be cremated but must be set afloat in the Ganges. The Aghori cult members fish them out and eat them. When not so occupied, the numerous Aghori can be seen scooping up cow droppings with human skulls for another aspect of their unpleasant diet.

ఆర్(రా)ఎం

THE TURNING OF THE BONES

Every second year in Madagascar the locals get ready for Famadihana, or The Turning of the Bones. They believe that the quicker the body decomposes, the quicker the spirit gets to the afterlife, so everybody digs up their departed and dances the corpses round big fires while bands play a merry tune. The dead are then reburied – until next time.

တတ်ဌာ

A BLOODY FESTIVAL

The innocuous sounding Vegetarian Festival of Phuket in Thailand is a bit of a stomach-turner. Having given themselves a good whipping, Thais then slash at their bodies with assorted blades, split their tongues and compete to see who can stick the most blades through their faces.

တတ်ဌာ

THE ORIGINAL BUNGEE JUMP

Pentecost Island in the Pacific holds the annual Gol. Young males have to make vine ropes of exactly the right length, allowing for stretch and their own body length, attach these to their ankles and dive head first from a 100-foot tower to come within 3 inches of the ground. Australians have since adopted the ritual as bungee jumping.

တတ်ဌာ

THE PEOPLE'S TEMPLE OF CALIFORNIA

One of the darkest cults ever was the People's Temple of California. In 1977 founder James Jones took his 'flock' off to Guyana to establish Jonestown, proclaiming they would all one day die together and be 'translated' to another planet. In 1978, having ordered the slaughter of a congressional delegation come to see what he was up to, Jones told his flock it was Translation Time. All 909 took cyanide to follow him to paradise.

THE DEVIL'S LEAP

On Corpus Christi Day, the Spanish town of Castrillo de Murcia holds the Devil's Leap. All the newborn babies are laid out together on large mattresses so that men dressed as the devil can leap over them to purge them of Original Sin. There have been the inevitable tragedies caused by ill-timed jumps and drunken 'devils' but despite Benedict XVI calling for a ban, the ritual continues.

A BIG DAY IN KOMAKI

Japan celebrate Big Penis Day on 15 March every year. A ten-foot wooden phallus is carried through the town by selected volunteers to ensure fecundity among the locals, and after through the fields to ensure the fertility of crops in the approaching spring.

16 GLORIOUS FOOD FACTS

1. In Japan sake means liquor and can denote any type of alcohol. That which Westerners call sake is in Japan called *seishu*, and it is not a rice wine but a beer.

2. Perhaps the French are so fond of cheese because the food contains naturally occurring morphine from cows' milk.

3. Peru is the only country in the world in which Coca-Cola is outsold by another soft drink – Inca-Kola, which apparently tastes like bubblegum.

4. In the general Western mind, sushi is raw fish but the term actually means sour-tasting and refers instead to the preparation of food with vinegar-flavoured rice.

5. Eggs boiled in virgins' urine is a popular delicacy in Dongyang, China; cats, dogs and monkeys are also great delicacies.

6. Until Prohibition ended in Iceland on 1 March 1989, Icelanders drank more Coca-Cola per capita than any other nation.

7. Short of money but keen to have Pepsi expand its operation in their country, Russia gave the company seventeen submarines, a cruiser, a frigate and a destroyer. Until Pepsi sold them for scrap to liquidize the assets, the company had the distinction of running the ninth largest fleet of submarines in the world.

8. Of no fixed recipe, chicken tikka masala is a British dish 'invented' in 1963 in the Shish Mahal curry house in Glasgow's West End.

9. About 10 per cent of the Russian Treasury's revenue comes from tax on vodka.

10. Caesar salad is named after Caesar Cardini who ran a chain of restaurants along the US/Mexican border. It was first presented to customers to celebrate Independence Day in 1925.

11. Red Bull is banned in several countries as it is laced with glucuronolactone, a mood-enhancing stimulant used by American troops in the Vietnam War.

12. Until the BSE scare, cow-brain burgers were popular in the US, where it is now illegal to sell the brains of cows older than thirty months at slaughter.

13. The larvae of ants infesting the roots of the agave plant are a popular snack in Mexico. Served up raw with a little salsa, they are known as insect caviar.

14. Icelanders are big on *hákarl*. First catch your shark, bury it in the back garden for three or four months and then dig it up and snack out on the raw meat!

15. In Cambodia, *a-ping* is a popular street snack. Live tarantulas are dusted with sugar and garlic powder before being deep-fried until the legs are stiff but the abdomen is still runny inside.

16. Nothing beats *ikizukuri* for brutality. Japanese customers choose their fish from a tank so the chef can gut it live at the table before speedily hacking at the body so it can be eaten alive with the heart still beating.

QUIZ 4

A   Switzerland hosted the first Eurovision Song Contest – who won?

B   What did bush pilot Jimmy Angel discover when flying over Venezuela in 1939?

C   Which country employs train ushers to push passengers into already crowded trains?

D   Where in the world can you be flogged for spitting out chewing gum onto the pavement?

E   Which island group of British protection has a population of 3,000, with 500,000 sheep?

F   Which country has the greatest population of wild camels?

G   Which country of the northern hemisphere has over 3 million lakes?

H   The population of which Mediterranean island nation is outnumbered 2:1 by nationals living abroad?

I   Which country is the largest producer of opium?

J   Which country has the largest prison population?

K   Which language famously only has twelve letters in its alphabet?

L   Which is the only country to list subscribers by their first names in the telephone books?

M   Which country has the most pyramids?

ANSWERS TO QUIZ 4 *NOT SO EASY — YOU'LL NEED A MIRROR TO CHECK THESE OUT!*

A   The host nation won the competition.

B   Angel Falls, the highest waterfall in the world.

C   Japan.

D   Singapore.

E   The Falkland Islands.

F   Australia.

G   Canada.

H   Malta.

I   Afghanistan.

J   The USA.

K   Hawaiian.

L   Iceland.

M   Sudan.

THE NATURAL WORLD

VOLCANOES: 13 EXPLOSIVE FACTS

1. There are about 1,500 active volcanoes on the surface of the earth with perhaps 100,000 more under the sea.

2. Most submarine volcanic eruptions go unnoticed as they occur at depths in excess of 2,000 metres.

3. There are 10,000 active volcanoes under the Pacific Ocean alone, with the largest of these being the Tamu Massif.

4. In the movies lava travels as a slow menace but, in reality and depending on the terrain, lava can set a fair pace, reaching up to speeds of 40 mph.

DID YOU KNOW?

The Kīlauea volcano in Hawaii has been in constant eruption since 1983.

5. On Hawaii, the now-dormant Mauna Kea is the tallest volcano on earth, measuring over 33,000 feet from its submarine base to apex – twice the height of Everest.

6. Italy's Mount Etna has been active for the past 3,500 years – the first documented eruption came in 1500 BC and the most recent, at the time of writing, shut down Italian air traffic in June 2014.

7. More dangerous than volcanoes are magma pits, the largest known lying in America's Yellowstone Park. An underground chamber full of lava, it is over 55 miles long, 18 miles wide in places and runs to depths of over 9 miles.

8. The maleo bird of Indonesia buries its eggs in hot sand near active volcanoes to let the geothermic heat do the hatching.

9. Because Australia sits right in the middle of a massive tectonic plate it has never had any volcanoes.

10. Far more dangerous than the lava flow is the blast of volcanic pyroclastic gas, which reaches temperatures of 2,000°F and travels at ground level at speeds of up to 700 kph.

11. When lava cools and sets it becomes pumice, the only rock that will float.

12. The largest volcano so far discovered lurks under the Pacific Ocean to the east of Japan. Measuring 650 kilometres across, the Tamu Massif is about the size of the UK.

13. The world's smallest volcano is Mexico's Cuexcomate, located just outside the city of Puebla. It stands at a mere 43 feet with a base diameter of just 75 feet.

DID YOU KNOW?

Brazil got its name from the nuts that grow there – not the other way round.

Toilet Trivia The magician John Nevil Maskelyne invented the coin-operated lock for public lavatories in 1892.

MYTH BUSTERS

- Unlike the old saying, lightning does strike in the same place. The Empire State Building takes about 100 hits a year.

- Oak trees do not produce acorns until they are at least fifty years old.

- A coin dropped from a tall structure will not kill anyone below. It lacks sufficient mass and, tumbling in descent, does not acquire enough momentum.

- Not since the Middle Ages has it been possible for the world's population to squeeze onto the Isle of Wight.

- Despite what you see in the movies, you cannot drown in quicksand nor even sink below the surface, no matter how deep it is.

- If anyone tells you it is too cold for snow, send them to Antarctica.

- Sea level is not a fixed benchmark as it depends on location, time of day, local rainfall and a host of other factors.

- No Inuit ever lived in an igloo – they are temporary shelters built by hunters on the move. Fewer than 4 per cent of the Inuit have even seen one.

- Nor do the Inuit have twenty-eight words for 'snow'. They have three: one for falling snow, one for fallen snow and another for snow that sticks.

DID YOU KNOW?

The Statue of Liberty was originally designed as a Muslim woman, traditionally attired, to stand at the northern entrance of the Suez Canal but the Khedive of Egypt changed his mind so the French 'tweaked' the design and gave it to America.

WATER, WATER, EVERYWHERE

About 90 per cent of the world's fresh water is
locked in the Antarctic ice caps.

❖

Not all rivers flow to the sea; many drain into lakes,
swamps or wetlands.

❖

There is enough water in Lake Superior alone to
cover both North and South America a foot deep.

❖

Each cubic mile of fog contains over 56,000
gallons of water.

❖

Saudi Arabia, Yemen, Oman, Qatar and the United Arab
Emirates don't have a single river between them.

❖

At 3,212 feet, Venezuela's Angel Falls is the highest
waterfall in the world, fifteen times higher than
Niagara.

❖

The Amazon river is not the longest river in the
world but carries four times as much water into the
Atlantic as any other river.

❖

Toilet Trivia — Loo flushing accounts for about 25 per cent of the water usage in the average home.

10 per cent of the world's plastic output ends up in the oceans and the two largest garbage dumps in the world float in the Pacific.

❖

Across rural Africa and Asia people have to walk an average of 4 miles every day to collect fresh water.

❖

In summer, the average swimming pool loses 1,000 gallons a month to evaporation.

❖

31 per cent of your bone mass is actually water.

❖

Pure water will not conduct electricity – only water containing impurities can do that.

❖

Lake Baikal in Russia is the largest in the world and contains over 20 per cent of the world's unfrozen drinkable water.

❖

The expiry date on bottled water is not for the water but for the bottle; that is the date on which the plastic will start leaching chemicals into its contents.

❖

At the top of Everest, the boiling point of water drops to 71 degrees centigrade.

❖

Commonly known as the Mpemba Effect, under certain conditions hot water will freeze faster than cold.

❖

In the US, 40 per cent of the freshwater demand goes to agriculture. This rises to 65 per cent in China, 94 per cent in Pakistan, Cambodia and Vietnam and 97 per cent in Madagascar.

❖

Capable of dissolving countless elements and compounds, water is the most common and effective solvent on the planet.

DID YOU KNOW?

If you run through a downpour you stay about 40 per cent drier than those who walk.

8 NATURAL DISASTERS

1. A freak heatwave in January 1919 ruptured the molasses storage tanks in Boston, unleashing 2.5 million gallons of the stuff. It travelled in a 25-foot-high wave that killed or injured over 200 people and hundreds of tethered horses.

2. In 1952 unusually high-pressure systems settled over London to trap pollution at ground level. Over 5,000 died of respiratory and cardiac conditions in the Great Smog and the Clean Air Act was pushed through in 1956.

3. Weighing up to a kilo, hailstones can be lethal. In 1888 such a storm hit Uttar Pradesh to kill over 300 people and 2,000 animals. In 1984 a similar storm hit Munich to injure thousands and write off over 200,000 cars.

4. In the summer of 2010 the normally tranquil waters off the southern French coast erupted with 40-foot-high waves that smashed into the coast between Cannes and Nice. It destroyed countless cafes and seafront businesses, just before the film festival was scheduled to begin.

5. A massive earthquake caused by the Dead Sea fault system in 1138 levelled the city of Aleppo in Syria, causing around 230,000 deaths.

6. In 1976 the Chinese industrial city of Tangshan found itself at the epicentre of a massive quake that killed over two-thirds of the densely packed population of more than a million.

7. At 9.20 a.m. on the morning of 15 February 2013 a meteor entered the earth's atmosphere over Chelyabinsk in Russia. Travelling at about 42,000 mph, or sixty times the speed of sound, it put out shockwaves detected 9,000 miles away. Although it passed 18 miles above the earth, it still managed to release over thirty Hiroshimas-worth of energy to cause widespread damage and the hospitalisation of over 1,500 people.

8. On Boxing Day 2010 a 1,000-mile-long fault shuddered under the Indian Ocean. The resulting tsunami killed over 300,000 people in fourteen countries, with the last fatalities being two tourists in South Africa swept off the beach twelve hours after the initial event.

 **Toilet Trivia** On average, a person uses around 20,800 sheets of toilet paper every year.

NATURE'S NUTRITION

The largest living entity is a 4 sq mi mushroom
wheel in Oregon's Blue Mountains.

❧

Peanuts are used in the manufacture of dynamite.

❧

Bananas, avocados, tomatoes and melons all go
off quicker in the fridge.

❧

Until the Victorians, chocolate was only a drink.

❧

Pound for pound, crisps are seventy times the cost
of potatoes.

❧

Red peppers are just ripened green ones.

❧

Nutmeg can be lethal if taken intravenously.

❧

The high potassium content of bananas makes
them ever so slightly radioactive.

❧

Almonds are not nuts but hard seeds.

QUIZ 5

A   The name of which mountain means the Ogre?

B   Name the deepest point in the oceans.

C   Where is consistently the hottest place on the planet?

D   Ireland's Giant's Causeway comprises interlocking columns of which rock?

E   What is the largest structure made up of living entities?

F   By what name is Rapa Nui better known?

G   Name the most northern, southern, western and eastern of the American states.

H   What is the name of the largest mountain range?

I   What do you always find after lightening hits a beach?

J   Which European city has the greatest mileage of canals within its boundaries?

K   Because it was used to dilate ladies' pupils, which plant was named 'beautiful woman'?

L   How many times can the same paper be recycled?

M   Name the highest capital city in Europe.

N   What is unusual about the wood known as lignum vitae?

O   In New Zealand what are outnumbered 20:1 by sheep?

ANSWERS TO QUIZ 5 — NOT SO EASY – YOU'LL NEED A MIRROR TO CHECK THESE OUT!

A   The Eiger.

B   The Mariana Trench in the Pacific – it is just short of seven miles deep.

C   Death Valley in California, which is also the lowest and driest point in America.

D   Basalt.

E   The Great Barrier Reef.

F   Easter Island.

G   Hawaii to the south and, with the world being round, Alaska takes the other accolades.

H   The Oceanic Ridge that runs for 35,000 miles through the Atlantic, Pacific and Indian Oceans.

I   Glass.

J   Birmingham, which has Venice beat by about 3 miles.

K   Belladonna.

L   Six times – after that the fibres are too weak.

M   Madrid.

N   It is so dense that it sinks in water.

O   People.

NOW AND THEN: HISTORY'S BEST BITS

UNCONVENTIONAL POPES

JOHN XII (955-64)

A self-professed atheist, John XII turned the papal residence into one of the wildest brothels in history and, when not whoring and gambling, he could be found trying to summon the Devil. He was finally clubbed to death in his bed by the husband of the woman he was raping at the time. Maintaining the family tradition, John XIII (965-72) was beaten to death in the middle of an adulterous liaison, just like his dear old dad.

⁂

STEPHEN VI (896-7)

Stephen VI exhumed his predecessor, Pope Formosus, and put his rotting corpse on trial for a shopping list of charges. Having conducted an abysmal self-defence, the corpse was dragged through the streets and chucked in the River Tiber. Realising the folly of their choice, the cardinals dragged Stephen into a dungeon and strangled him.

∽↺⊚↻∾

BENEDICT IX
(THREE TERMS BETWEEN 1032-48)

Benedict IX's first of three terms (1032-44) began, according to some reports, when he was only twelve. He soon proved himself a voracious sinner, dabbling in the black arts and sodomizing pilgrims of either sex. Tiring of the restriction his job put on his busy social life, he sold the papal throne to his godfather, who became Gregory VI.

∽↺⊚↻∾

BONIFACE VIII (1294-1303)

Having possibly murdered his predecessor Celestine V, Boniface VIII – yet another atheist – was eventually tried in absentia for heresy, rape, sodomy and, worst of all, eating meat during Lent.

∽↺⊚↻∾

JOHN XXII (1410-15)

The only (known) pirate Pope and regarded by the Catholic Church as an antipope. Having taken holy orders a mere day before ascending the throne, he was charged in 1415 with nearly one hundred counts of murder, piracy, rape and incest, prompting him to flee Rome for Germany, where he died in 1419.

PIUS II (1458-64)

Previously a published writer of pornographic literature, Pius is known to have fathered at least a dozen illegitimate children during his reign.

❧

PAUL II (1464-71)

Nicknamed Our Lady of Pity for his love of cross-dressing, he was another pope to go out with a bang, in his case carried off by a heart attack while being sodomized by one of his pages.

❧

SIXTUS IV (1471-84)

Builder of the Sistine Chapel, he was much enamoured of Rome's young male prostitutes, some of whom he promoted to the rank of cardinal to keep them close by. He created more cardinals than any other pope in history.

❧

ALEXANDER VI (1492-1503)

Also know as Rodrigo Borgia, probably the most infamous papal swinger of all time. He destroyed all Semitic images of Christ and had his equally repugnant son, Cesare, model for the white European image of Christ, still popular today. His reign of murder and depravity came to an end when he accidentally drank the poisoned wine he had prepared for an irksome cardinal.

JULIUS II (1503-13)

Responsible for commissioning the painting of the Sistine Chapel, he was a homosexual paedophile whose appetite for young boys knew no bounds.

֍

PAUL III (1534-49)

Famous for excommunicating Henry VIII for wishing to pursue his own lust, Paul III did not curtail his own. He also murdered countless people who stood in his way, including his own mother, and started a register of the city's prostitutes who had to pay him a monthly tribute to stay in business.

֍

JULIUS III (1550-55)

Another one for the young boys, Julius III still managed to raise a few eyebrows when he started an affair with the fifteen-year-old Bertuccino, his own illegitimate son.

֍

DID YOU KNOW?

Popes Hormisdas (514-23), Adrian II (867-72) and John XVII (May–November 1003) were all married when they took the job.

WHAT THE ROMANS DID

Made their soldiers pay for all their own gear.

❖

The ruling elite thought Latin common and spoke
Greek instead.

❖

They brushed their teeth with stale urine.

❖

A female fighter in the arena was called a gladiatrix.

❖

They thought that drinking gladiators' blood would
cure epilepsy.

❖

Ancient Rome was eight times more densely
populated than New York.

❖

On average, they lived until they were thirty-five.

❖

They used hallucinogenics as recreational drugs.

❖

Gladiators actually fought under strict rules and
rarely died.

THE FRENCH REVOLUTION: MYTHS, RESTAURANTS AND FROGS

FROGS AND TOADS

Harking back to the glory of the Frankish Kingdom and its heraldic device of three golden toads, it was common for the courtiers at Versailles to refer to themselves as toads and to the Parisians as frogs (they being the lesser of the two creatures). 'What do the Frogs say?' was a popular way of inquiring about the mood of Paris in pre-Revolutionary Versailles. Foreign visitors acquired the term and applied it to any Frenchman.

✲

AN UNNATURAL VIOLATION

You could say that the Marquis de Sade helped to start the French Revolution after shouting from his Bastille prison window about whippings and 'unnatural violation'. Believing his imaginings to be an account of what was actually happening inside, the mob attacked but only found six prisoners. In fact, the Bastille was already scheduled for demolition.

DID YOU KNOW?

The Vatican banks are reputed to launder such vast amounts of ill-gotten gains for the Mafia that the US State Department lists the Vatican as 'a country of concern'.

DR GUILLOTIN

Beheading machines were nothing new in 1789; they had been in use in England as early as 1286 in Halifax and were common across Europe. Dr Guillotin campaigned for the machine to be made available to commoners, who at the time had various painful and inefficient methods of dispatch while beheading was a luxury reserved for the nobility.

⌒⌒⌒

AN UNBALANCED DIET

'Revolution' describes something going full cycle to return to the point at which it started and so it was for the French *homme dans la rue* (man in the street) under the new administration. Although the movies depict an endless line of power-wigged fops flouncing off to the guillotine, the machine's diet was otherwise. Of those she devoured, 6 per cent were clergy, only 8 per cent were aristocrats and a huge 72 per cent were commoners.! *Plus* ça *change!*

⌒⌒⌒

SHORT AND SWEET

Marie Antoinette never uttered the callous 'Let them eat cake' during the pre-Revolutionary bread riots but she was hated nevertheless. On her last night in prison she summoned her executioner and paid him a full purse of gold to ensure the blade was good and sharp, so she could be certain of a clean death.

⌒⌒⌒

BON APPETIT

With only a few aristos gone, Paris was still left teeming with out-of-work flunkies and chefs who got together to do the only thing they knew well – how to cook and serve food. *Voilà la restaurant!* Prior to the Revolution there were no walk-in dining establishments anywhere in Europe. And the first to sample the delights of such pampering were, of course, the leading lights of the Revolution.

ᴄᴓᴓᴃ

PUTTING THE 'TERROR' IN TERRORISM

As a word and as a concept, the terrorism with which we all now live was born in the Revolution's so called Reign of Terror (September 1793 to July 1794). Known in France as *La Terreur*, or *La Terrorisme*, this was when Robespierre used state terrorism to disorientate and suppress any that opposed him. It was this horror that would later inspire Dickens' famous opening line from *A Tale of Two Cities*: 'It was the best of times, it was the worst of times.'

Toilet Trivia In 1890 the Scott Paper Company of Philadelphia became the first to market loo paper on a roll.

20 HISTORICAL FACTS YOU DIDN'T LEARN AT SCHOOL

1. Many recordings of Churchill's wartime speeches are the work of BBC voice actor Norman Shelley, later famous as Colonel Danby in *The Archers*. Churchill was just too busy with the war to go to the studios.

2. During the Nazi occupation of Paris, Coco Chanel was the mistress of Gestapo officer Hans von Dincklage, for whom she spied as Agent F-7124.

3. When the Viking Eric the Red discovered a new frozen wasteland, he named it Greenland to attract settlers.

4. In 1960, Fred and Wilma Flintstone became the first couple allowed to appear in bed together on American television.

5. The open stone stairs in medieval castles always spiralled anticlockwise so right-handed invaders would have their sword arm impeded by the wall, while defenders had full sweep.

6. The washing machine gave the West the Chinese takeaway. The advent of affordable domestic machines drove the Chinese laundries to the wall so the owners turned to their next best talent.

7. Napoleon was not short but of average height – so much for the so-called Napoleon complex.

8. When the *Mona Lisa* was stolen in 1911, painter Pablo Picasso was the prime suspect. It later transpired that an Italian thief called Vincenzo Peruggia had simply walked out with it tucked under his arm.

9. Santa Anna, the victor at the Alamo who was later defeated by Sam Houston, got his own back by starting the chewing-gum business in the US. His first product, Chiclets, is still in production.

10. Henry VIII and Elizabeth I both imposed taxes on beards, with Peter the Great of Russia doing likewise in 1698.

Toilet Trivia

The first flushing loo was invented in 1596 by Sir John Harrington, who installed it at Richmond Palace for his godmother, Elizabeth I.

11. The German newspaper *Die Zeitung* was published in the UK throughout the Second World War with a circulation of about 25,000.

12. In the closing airport scene of *Casablanca*, the man turning the propeller in the background was Rafael Trujillo, later the ruler and butcher of the Dominican Republic.

13. The shortest war in history was fought between Britain and Zanzibar. In 1896 the pro-British sultan died to be replaced by his anti-British son, who tore up all his father's agreements. The British sent in gunboats and war was declared at 9.02 on the morning of 27 August. It was over by 9.40.

14. Hitler was not a vegetarian; he loved sausages and game pie, and his favourite meal was stuffed pigeon. He only cut out meat when his notorious flatulence went into overdrive.

15. The first prime minster of the UK was Sir Henry Campbell-Bannerman as the title did not officially exist until 1905, just after he took office. All his predecessors were First Lords of the Treasury.

16. The year before Lincoln's assassination, his son Todd was pulled from the path of a train at New Jersey station. His saviour was Edwin Booth, brother of his father's killer.

17. Before he signed the embargo on Cuban cigars, JFK sent out for 200 boxes for the White House.

18. Denied access to cotton supplies during the First World War, the German army uniforms were woven from nettle fibres.

19. In 1938, Hitler was voted Man of the Year by *Time* magazine.

20. The last prisoners to be held in the Tower of London were the Kray brothers after they went AWOL in 1952 during their National Service.

FAMOUS CROSS-DRESSERS IN HISTORY

JOAN OF ARC (1412-31)

The so-called Joan of Arc was not French but born in the independent Duchy of Bar in 1412 (not part of France until 1766) and her name was closer to Jehanne Darc, though there is still some debate amongst scholars. Her 'Rouenation' was imposed not for her being deemed a witch, as is popularly told, but for the heresy of habitually wearing men's clothes, which was proscribed by the Bible. After she was beatified in 1909, French women started to copy her page-boy haircut and thus was born the popular 'bob cut'.

⤜⤙⤛⤚

DR JAMES BARRY (1795-1865)

This famed medical man also had a distinguished army career, rising to the post of Inspector General of British military hospitals. He fought duels and was perceived as 'one for the ladies', always flirting outrageously at balls. But on his death, Barry turned out to be a woman who had given birth to at least one child. Influential even after death, following the burial with full military honours in London's Kensal Green Cemetery, unmarked carriages descended on his home to remove all his papers and his war record vanished from the War Office.

⤜⤙⤛⤚

QUEEN CHRISTINA OF SWEDEN (1626-89)

Portrayed in film as a pouting vamp of passion by Garbo, Queen Christina of Sweden was in reality decidedly butch. In 1654, she abdicated and quit Sweden, dressed as a man. Possibly a hermaphrodite with more of a fondness for women than men, she roamed Europe and, upon her death, became one of the few women to be buried in St Peter's Basilica in Rome. She was exhumed in 1965 in an attempt to determine her true gender, but by then there was not much left to check out.

෴

J. EDGAR HOOVER (1895-1972)

The first director of the FBI ran the bureau with sinister efficiency while enjoying a long-term relationship with his aide, Clyde Tolson. Hoover was also a regular at the gay orgies held in a secluded suite in New York's Plaza Hotel. According to Susan, fourth wife of bisexual whisky baron Lewis Rosenstiel, Hoover always attended in drag, full makeup and a wig.

෴

CHARLES D'EON (1728-1810)

The Chevalier Charles D'Eon was one of Louis XV's best spies. Dressed as the Lady de Beaumont, he took up the post of Maid of Honour to the Empress Elizabeth of Russia in order to report back on court affairs and intrigues. 'Her' fencing abilities and gung-ho equestrian skills attracted many admirers among the Russian nobility, none of whom managed to make it past first base, for obvious reasons.

10 SECRETS OF THE NOT-SO-WILD WEST

1. Only the brave called someone a cowboy to their face in the American West. As today, the term was highly pejorative. 'Drover' was most commonly used.

2. The average age of drovers was sixteen and few made it past thirty, mostly dying from pneumonia, riding accidents or stampedes. None carried pistols as they simply couldn't afford them.

3. You were seventeen times more likely to be gunned down in London or New York, where people *could* afford guns, than in the American West.

4. No one ever faced off in Main Street at high noon and no lone gunslinger ever held an entire town in thrall. The inaccurate ammunition didn't help, and those comfortable with creeping up behind someone in the dark with a shotgun seem to have done best in the West.

DID YOU KNOW?

The city already depopulated by the plague, only six people died in the Great Fire of London.

5. In the so-called 'Gunfight at the O.K. Corral' – which actually took place on a vacant lot beside a boarding house – only thirty shots were fired in as many seconds, leaving three dead.

6. Billy the Kid was not a left-handed gun; the popular picture of him was taken from an accidentally reversed negative. He only killed three people, not the twenty-three of legend, before being gunned down himself.

7. Between 1840 and 1860 over 500,000 settlers traipsed through the Indian Territories, with about 360 killed in confrontations, mainly of their own instigation. Three times that number were stomped to death by their own livestock.

8. The wagon trains' main worry was well-armed white raiders. The worst attack ever was the Mountain Meadows Massacre of 1857, when the Baker-Fancher train was attacked by the good Mormons of Utah and 128 travellers lost their lives.

9. The American Indian is often touted as the ultimate eco-human but most bison hunts involved the setting of massive prairie fires to drive entire herds over cliffs, after which just the tongues were cut out as a delicacy.

10. American Indians did not communicate by smoke signals. A fire might be lit to confirm a previous verbal message, for example, but no one could waft a blanket over a fire to send up messages in puffs of smoke that others could 'read', like some sort of code.

THE VIKINGS...

Did not wear horned helmets.

❖

Sometimes fought naked.

❖

Drank from skulls – hence the beer brand Skol!

❖

Settled in America in the early tenth century.

❖

Were obsessively clean.

❖

Wore makeup in battle.

❖

Were mostly farmers, not raiders.

❖

Used magnetic compasses.

❖

Made human sacrifices at funerals, and to appease
their gods.

❖

Occupied Normandy, aka Land of the Norsemen.

CLEOPATRA: QUEEN OF THE NILE

WHO WAS SHE?

'Cleopatra' was more of a title than a name. Translating from the Greek as 'glory of the father', the most famous person to carry the title, and the one that we tend to mean when we talk about Cleopatra, was Thea Philopater, Cleopatra VII (69-30 BC). Despite being Pharaoh of Egypt, she spoke Greek, dressed in the Greek style and never mastered the language of her people.

⌘

DRESSING UP

Because she and all the other Cleopatras were perceived in Egypt as kings, she had to dress up as a man on state occasions; she even had to wear a silly stick-on beard.

⌘

NO BEAUTY QUEEN

Always depicted as some sort of exotic vamp, it has to be said that the lady was no beauty. Images of her that have survived show a hooked nose, a rather mean little mouth, a narrow forehead and a protruding chin.

⌘

EXTRAMARITAL AFFAIR

During one of her husband's (the famous Roman general Mark Antony) protracted visits to Rome, Cleopatra made overtures to Herod the Great, the king of Judea. According to the Jewish–Roman historian Josephus, the woman referred to as Cleopatra of Jerusalem was none other than Cleopatra VII, with the pair even producing a son called Philip.

⋐᷒᷒᷒᷒᷒ᷓ

THE FINAL ACT

One story goes that after the Egyptians' defeat at Actium (31 BC) she readily agreed to Octavian's demands for her to kill Antony so she could retain the throne. She summoned Antony and, having convinced him she had already taken poison, she sat and watched as he fell on his sword. Only when she learned that Octavian actually intended to drag her through the streets of Rome in chains did she *really* take poison.

⋐᷒᷒᷒᷒᷒ᷓ

QUIZ 6

A In the famous Shakespearean quote, which English king would have been happy to exchange his kingdom for a horse?

B Who was born in Argentina in 1928 as Ernesto Lynch?

C During the Second World War, which nation was attacked in Operation Barbarossa?

D Why did British farmers abandon the traditional purple carrot in favour of orange ones in 1689?

E Where was Napoleon born?

F What did William II, Charles I and George VI all have in common?

G By what nickname was William Henry McCarty best known?

H Which famous writer helped organize and mobilize the Spanish Armada?

I The warrior Shaka founded which kingdom in 1818?

J During the eighteenth century, which commodity was most regularly smuggled into England?

K Whose mistress was Claretta Petacci?

L The battle cry of 'Tora! Tora! Tora!' is associated with which engagement?

M How many times was Henry VIII divorced?

N Who famously wrote, 'I do not trust any Russian'?

ANSWERS TO QUIZ 6

NOT SO EASY — YOU'LL NEED A MIRROR TO CHECK THESE OUT!

A   Richard III.

B   Che Guevara.

C   The Soviet Union was attacked by Germany.

D   To celebrate William of Orange coming over to ascend the throne.

E   Corsica – he never did master French.

F   They all had pronounced stutters.

G   Billy the Kid; William Bonney was just an alias he used.

H   Cervantes.

I   The Zulu Kingdom.

J   Tea.

K   Mussolini's.

L   The Japanese attack on Pearl Harbour.

M   None – he sorted out his marital problems with annulments or the axe.

N   Karl Marx.

CRIME AND PUNISHMENT: THE LONG ARM OF THE LAW

OLD SPARKY: DEATH BY ELECTROCUTION

THE DENTIST CHAIR

The electric chair was invented in 1889 by New York dentist Alfred Southwick, who used his surgery chair as a model. Unveiling his brainchild, he pronounced: 'We live in a higher civilization from this day.' First to go to the chair was Willie Kemmler (d. 6 August 1890) who took eight minutes to die. After the third attempt to ensure death, most witnesses fled the chamber as Willie burst into flames.

ACCIDENTAL DEATH

American army executioner Sergeant John C. Woods, who hanged the Nazis after the Nuremberg Trials, accidentally dispatched himself on 21 July 1950 while making repairs to an engineer lighting set in the Marshall Islands.

৩৩৩৩

SHORT-CIRCUIT

In old movies the prison lights were always shown to dim and flicker when Old Sparky was turned on. In fact, the chair operates on a massive short-circuit so it is impossible for it to be connected to the ordinary supply. Talking of that short-circuit, it is frequently told that Emperor Menelik II of Ethiopia ordered an electric chair in 1898 to 'modernize' his execution programme but none could get it to function on the normal supply – so he had it upholstered and used it as his throne.

৩৩৩৩

MIRACULOUS ESCAPES

At Sing Sing in 1932, murderer James Bullen was pronounced dead in the chair but recovered en route to the cemetery. He leapt out of his coffin to make a run for it but was caught and taken back for a second go. On 3 May 1936, Willie Francis was also found to have survived his electrocution, which had been botched by a drunken guard in Louisiana. His lawyers instigated appeal proceedings but on 9 May 1947 Willie went back to the chair. He was eighteen when he died.

SWINGING BRITAIN

Known as the Bloody Code, in eighteenth-century Britain 222 offences invited death by hanging. Here are a few of the more trivial:

Consorting with gypsies.

❖

Writing a threatening letter.

❖

Appearing on the King's Highway with a blacked-up face.

❖

Stealing anything worth more than 12 pence.

❖

Impersonating a Chelsea pensioner.

❖

Writing on or otherwise defacing Westminster Bridge.

❖

Setting fire to a haystack.

❖

Any poaching.

❖

Cutting down a tree for firewood.

DON'T GIVE UP THE DAY JOB: CRIMINAL INCOMPETENCE

THE JOURNAL

On 14 March 2002 Patrick Daniel was pulled over by Utah police for not having number plates. Concerned by a journal found in Daniel's car, which had entries reminding him to 'torch car' and 'bury in a remote area', the officers opened the trunk to find the bodies of Robert Bilton and Beckie Britton.

❦

PROFESSIONAL BUNGLER

Having crashed his getaway car in 1971, professional burglar Rodney Dobson was in court for the forty-third time. Handing down an eighteen-month sentence, the judge told Dobson, 'You should give up burglary: you have a withered arm, one false leg and only one eye. You are a useless burglar.'

❦

AN UNWELCOME VISITOR

In 2002 a handbag thief was being chased by security staff at South Africa's Bloemfontein Zoo when he decided to take a shortcut through the tigers' enclosure – a journey he failed to complete.

❦

CAUGHT SHORT

In December 1983 police interrupted a theatre performance of *Snow White and the Seven Dwarfs* to arrest Raymond McCray on stage for his botched robbery of an Ilford bank. At 3 feet 6 inches he was shorter than the counter so he thought the CCTV cameras would not 'see' him as he shouted instruction to the puzzled tellers who, seeing no robber, failed to stump up any cash. They only caught sight of McCray as he ran for the door.

❧

OUT FOR THE COUNT

In April 1998 Christina Mack was arrested for attempted murder in Peoria, Illinois. Having told her neighbours of her plans, she had greased the bathroom floor and the top of the stairs to kill Chester Parker, her one-legged partner. Mack slipped in her own trap and knocked herself out on the bath, Parker fell coming to her aid and the neighbours phoned the police who took away the still-unconscious Mack.

❧

SPEAK UP!

On 6 June 1995 a would-be bank robber walked into the Bank of Israel in Tel Aviv and whispered to a teller that he was there to rob the bank. The batteries in the teller's hearing aid had gone flat so she repeatedly told the robber he would have to speak up. Exasperated, the robber fled the premises.

❧

DOUBLE TROUBLE

In 2005 thieves burst into a Sacramento petrol station. Realizing the tills had been recently emptied, they gagged and tied up the staff, put up signs saying CASH ONLY and happily worked the station under the gaze of CCTV. The plan might have just worked had other thieves, attracted by the CASH ONLY signs, not robbed the first pair, who they then left tied up for the police to find.

MAX THE GORILLA

In 1997, having fallen from the roof of the luxury home he was trying to rob, Isaac Mofokeng fled though the crowds in Johannesburg Zoo, scaling a wall and swimming a moat to shake off the police. Pausing on the other side to make rude gestures at his smirking pursuers, Mofokeng turned to find himself face-to-face with Max, a 200-kilo gorilla who immediately sank his fangs into Isaac's buttocks and held on until the police and handlers came to take away his new friend.

A study showed that the first cubicle in a public toilet is always the least used – and therefore the cleanest.

LAST WORDS OF THE CONDEMNED

'That gas is going to play hell with my asthma.'

*Luis Monge (d. 2 june 1967) on his way to the
Colorado State Prison gas chamber.*

❖

'Shoot straight, you bastards, and don't fuck it up!'

*Australian Lieutenant Harry Morant (d. 27 February 1902) to
his own firing squad in South Africa during the Boer War.*

❖

'Not today!'

*Guy Fawkes (d. 31 January 1606), just before he threw himself
from the high platform where he was due to be hanged
and quartered. He broke his neck and died instantly.*

❖

'Such is life.'

*Ned Kelly (d. 11 November 1880) to his executioner
outside Melbourne Jail.*

❖

'Yes; hurry it up, you Hoosier [resident of Indiana]
bastard. I could hang a dozen men while you're
screwing around.'

*Mass murderer Carl Panzram (d. 5 December 1930) to his
executioner, who had just asked if he had any last words.*

❖

'Are you sure this thing is safe?'

*Mass poisoner Dr William Palmer (d. 14 June 1856) of
Staffordshire, while stamping on the trapdoor of his gallows.*

✤

'Yes; a bullet-proof vest!'

*James W. Rogers (d. 30 March 1960) when asked if he had any
last requests as he faced his firing squad in Utah State Prison.*

✤

'I did not get my Spaghetti Os, I just got spaghetti.
I want the press to know this.'

*Murderer Thomas J. Grasso (d. 20 March 1995) complaining
about his last meal on his way to lethal injection in
Oklahoma State Penitentiary.*

✤

'I'll be in Hell before you start breakfast, boys. Let
her rip!'

*Black Jack Ketchum (d. 26 April 1901), one-time associate
of Butch Cassidy and the Sundance Kid, just before
he was decapitated by his botched hanging.*

✤

'Gentlemen, I suggest you look away; this will
not be a pretty sight.'

*Mass murderer Dr Marcel Petiot (d. 25 May 1946) giving
advice to the witnesses who came to his guillotining in Paris.*

15 STRANGE LAWS

1. In the USA there are no federal laws prohibiting sex with animals. It is only illegal in seventeen of the states, with the other thirty-three states having no legislation at all.

2. Although British MPs are banned from wearing armour in Westminster, they can, within the House, commit arson, burglary, murder, deal drugs, make bombs and carry guns. They can also run a brothel and a casino. The law was last challenged in 1935 when it was upheld.

3. In San Salvador, first-time drunk drivers meet the firing squad – no second-time offenders there! In Bulgaria, second-time offenders risk execution.

4. If you are a bona fide traveller (more than seven miles from home) you can canter up to any pub in the UK that is licensed as an inn and demand admittance, no matter the hour. The licence holder is obliged to furnish you with stabling facilities, a simple meal and a bed for the night.

5. Under Section 43:21 of the Texas Penal Code, it used to be illegal for anyone to own more than six dildos. A recent class action mounted by Texas sex-shop owners was heard by the Fifth US Court of Appeals, which ruled the law unconstitutional.

6. In January 2015 Russia banned all transvestites and transsexuals from driving lest their 'flamboyant' appearance distract other drivers.

7. Singapore is a very clean city – perhaps because litterbugs can get a $5,000 fine and a Community Work Order. Failure to flush the loo after use and acts of petty vandalism attract equally hefty fines and a public caning to boot!

8. Vicks Inhalers are banned in Japan and you *will* be arrested if caught with one at the airport.

9. In Barbados it is illegal for anyone to wear camouflaged clothing or to even carry a bag presenting such a colour scheme.

10. Feeding the pigeons in Venice can get you a 500 euro fine, while in Nottingham in December 2014, pensioner Beryl Withers was threatened with a £2,000 fine for feeding her sandwich crumbs to local pigeons.

11. Contrary to popular perception, marijuana is illegal in Jamaica and being caught with even the smallest amount for personal use will land you in jail.

12. In the UAE and Saudi Arabia any public display of affection – even holding hands – will land you both in jail.

13. In Carmel, California, where Clint Eastwood once served as mayor, it is illegal for women to wear high heels; men can teeter around in them to their hearts' content, though.

14. Playing cards on Sunday can still get you six months' hard labour in Alabama, and in 1890 Illinois outlawed the playing of nine-pins and the sale of ice-cream sodas on a Sunday. People simply added another pin to create ten-pin bowling and, omitting the soda, added the coulis straight to the ice-cream 'sundae'.

15. In 1770 the UK passed a law stating that women 'seducing into marriage any of His Majesty's male subjects by the use of scents, paints, cosmetic washes, artificial teeth, false hair, Spanish wool, hoops, stays, high heels or bolstered hips shall incur the penalty of the law now in force against witchcraft'.

DID YOU KNOW?

On 18 February 1916, Father Hans Schmidt became the only priest executed in America for murder after he killed his pregnant lover, hacked her up and tossed the bits into New York's East River. He died in the chair in Sing Sing Prison.

QUIZ 7

A Which superhero first appeared as a telepathic villain bent on world domination?

B By what name is Richard Bingham better known?

C The Mafia live by the code of omertà; what does that mean?

D How many people did Machine Gun Kelly kill?

E The model for Dracula, Vlad Dracul, favoured which method of execution?

F Which of the Great Train Robbers was shot dead by his swimming pool in Spain?

G Which American criminal's middle name was Chestnut?

H Lew Wallace, who ordered the shooting of Billy the Kid, wrote which famous novel?

I Eugène Vidocq helped Sir Robert Peel set up which London police unit?

J Which American gangster campaigned for the first 'sell-by' dates on food?

K Mary Mallon, the most deadly cook in nineteenth-century America, was known by what nickname?

L Who was finally arrested in 1739 for drunkenly shooting chickens in the streets of York?

M Who was the last woman to be hanged in the UK?

ANSWERS TO QUIZ 7 *NOT SO EASY – YOU'LL NEED A MIRROR TO CHECK THESE OUT!*

A Superman in 1933.

B Lord 'Lucky' Lucan.

C Silence.

D None – he had a morbid fear of guns; the noise always scared him!

E Impaling on wooden stakes, hence his epithet of Vlad the Impaler.

F Charlie Wilson, shot by a cycling hit man in Marbella in 1990.

G Clyde Chestnut Barrow, he of Bonnie and Clyde fame.

H Ben Hur.

I Scotland Yard.

J Al Capone. He demanded legislation to put dates on milk bottles to make it better for schools.

K Typhoid Mary; a carrier of the disease who killed all who employed her.

L Dick Turpin – who never had a horse called Black Bess.

M Ruth Ellis in 1955.

SCIENCE: ALWAYS STRANGER THAN FICTION

10 MIND-BLOWING SCIENTIFIC FACTS

1. Glass is neither solid nor liquid but an amorphous solid. Left long enough on a solid surface, a glass tumbler would start to sag.

2. If you could find a big enough bowl of water, Saturn would float in it because the planet's density is so low.

3. Far from being muffled by fog, sound travels further and faster in it. The denser the environment the better.

4. With energy having mass, a litre of boiling water weighs fractionally more than a litre of cold.

5. After splitting the atom in 1917, Ernest Rutherford unwisely dismissed the energy release as weak and said that anyone hailing it as a source of power was out of their minds.

6. No apple fell on Isaac Newton's head to kick-start his theory of universal gravitation. The story was made up years later.

7. Water is the only substance on earth that is lighter in solid form than in liquid. Water expands as it freezes and is less dense, which is why ice floats in water.

8. Gorillas and potatoes have two more chromosomes than humans.

9. Humans instinctively suck skin injuries because their saliva contains a painkiller called opiorphin that is six times stronger than morphine.

10. Pound for pound, the gonorrhoea bacterium is the strongest organism on the planet, capable of dragging 100,000 times its own weight.

ROBOTS: FROM DA VINCI TO NASA

ROBOTA

The device recognized as the first robot was a steam-powered bird made by the Greek Archytas in about 400 BC. It could fly for 200 metres. Robot comes from the Czech 'robota' meaning slave labour, with 'robot' introduced into the English language by *Rossum's Universal Robots* (1921) by Karel Capek, a play that took London by storm. Naturally, the robots rebelled and killed everybody.

❧

A ROBOTIC KNIGHT

In 1495 Leonardo da Vinci designed a robotic knight and a robotic cart, the designs of which were copied by NASA for the surface droids exploring Mars. Only thought to be able to last ninety days on the Red Planet, those two robots were still exploring the surface six years later.

❧

DOMESTIC SERVICE

As early as the seventeenth century, Japan was using humanoid robots in domestic service – called *karakuri*, they would serve tea to guests. By the eighteenth century the *karakuri* were sophisticated enough to mime out entire plays.

✿

ELEKTRO

The first talking android was built in 1939 by Westinghouse. Called Elektro, it stood seven feet tall and had a vocabulary of 700 words. It was still functioning well enough in 1960 to star in trash-movie *Sex Kittens Go to College*.

✿

THE FIRST CYBORG

In 2015 Kevin Warwick, Professor of Cybernetics at Reading University, became the first cyborg after implanting microchips in his arm. He also implanted his wife's arm so he could feel whatever she touched when they were together.

DID YOU KNOW?

Einstein and Darwin both married their first cousins.

Toilet Trivia

Hitchcock's *Psycho* was the first film to show a toilet flushing, the scene causing outrage in America.

7 STRANGE EXPERIMENTS

1. Eighteenth-century physician Luigi Galvani, quickly bored of making frogs legs jerk about with electricity, soon moved on to human corpses. Touring Europe, he put on a show of the dead leaping about, inspiring Mary Shelley's *Frankenstein*.

2. In the 1950s, fascinated with the strategic possibilities of LSD, the CIA set up Operation Midnight Climax, which involved them running a string of brothels in California and New York. The punters were dosed with the drug and then filmed by hidden cameras. All in the interest of National Security, obviously.

3. The CIA MK-Ultra programme also experimented with using LSD as a weapon. It now seems the CIA was responsible for spraying the French village of Pont Saint Esprit with some kind of LSD cocktail in 1951. Everyone in the village went bonkers: fifty ended up in asylums and seven died after jumping out of windows.

4. In the 1970s the US Army set up a remote base to try to develop psychic Jedi warriors who could become invisible at will, walk through walls and kill their victims just by looking at them. Daft as it sounds, it really did happen and is the inspiration for the book and film *The Men Who Stare at Goats*.

5. In the late 1920s the Russian doctor Ilya Ivanov was hidden away in West Guinea where he was trying to produce a man-ape hybrid. Using both male and female 'volunteers' from the local population, some think him responsible for allowing simian AIDS to jump the species barrier.

6. In the 1950s biologist Hans Rieder spent two years soaking spiders in urine taken from schizophrenics and then studying the webs they wove, looking for erratic patterns. Results were inconclusive.

7. Invited in 1983 to lecture the American Urological Society on his experiments with erectile dysfunction, Dr Giles Brindley informed his audience that he himself had been suffering until he injected his penis with a vasodilatory drug. Then he dropped his trousers to show off the results.

DID YOU KNOW?

There are over 1.5 million industrial robots in use – over half of those in Japan.

DINO MYTHS

Dinosaur remains have been discovered all around the world for centuries, which explains the ubiquity of the notion of dragons from China through to Wales. But the dinosaurs themselves have evolved a few myths of their own:

The dinosaurs are not extinct; birds, from the tiny hummingbird to the ostrich, are in fact living dinosaurs.

❖

The pterodactyl was not a flyer but a glider that swooped and rose on thermals.

❖

The velociraptors of *Jurassic Park* are well wide of the mark. In reality they were about the size of a turkey and covered with feathers, not scales.

❖

Mammals lived quite happily alongside the dinosaurs for 150 million years, often snacking out on dinosaur eggs.

❖

Dinosaurs weren't slow-witted or slow-moving. Be they predator or prey, they were all pretty nippy – they had to be to survive.

❖

The dinosaurs were not evolutionary failures; they were around for 150 million years. We have been here for a scant 6 million years!

❖

It seems there was no one, single catastrophic event that saw off the dinosaurs, but rather a slow decline brought about by climatic and environmental changes.

❖

There's no such dinosaur as a Brontosaurus. What American palaeontologist Othniel Marsh unearthed in the nineteenth century was actually the body of an Apatosaurus along with the head of a Camarasaurus.

❖

Known in paleontological circles as the Flintstone Fallacy, the notion that dinosaurs and humans ever co-existed is a cinema-engendered myth.

❖

For years it was thought that the big sauropods such as the Apatosaurus spent their lives in the water to support their massive bulk. Wrong – they were land animals.

❖

The 'forearms' of T-Rex are always depicted as being puny and almost vestigial. Actually, those puny forearms could lift about a ton.

IT'S ALL FICTION:
PHYSICS IN THE MOVIES

KNIFE THROWING

It is impossible for anyone to throw a knife with sufficient force for it to embed to the hilt in a human body. The crucial factors of mass and velocity are simply not there.

෧෧෨෨

THE SILENT GUN

Putting a pillow over a gun or firing it through a 2-litre plastic bottle will not act as a silencer. In fact, there is no such thing as a cigar-sized silencer that will reduce the noise of gunfire to a muted 'phutt'. Modern ammunition is hypersonic so nothing fitted to the muzzle is going to eliminate the crack of the bullet breaking the sound barrier.

෧෧෨෨

THE FORCE OF A BULLET

No one gets knocked through a plate-glass window by gunfire, not even from both barrels of a heavy-gauge shotgun. The ammunition simply does not have the mass and Newton's Third Law of Motion decrees that this would only be possible if the shooter was flung back with equal force.

෧෧෨෨

DID YOU KNOW?

In 2011 a mass of water was discovered just floating in space; the estimated volume is equivalent to about 140 trillion times that of all the water on earth.

THE DEADLY CIGARETTE

The sneering villain's discarded cigarette tumbles slow-mo into a petrol flood to instigate a homicidal conflagration. It can't happen: the cigarette would be extinguished. Dr Richard Tontarski, forensic fire expert with the American BATF, failed to provoke ignition after 2,000 attempts.

GREAT BALLS OF FIRE

A well-aimed shot at the rear of a fleeing car and the petrol tank explodes. This might be achieved with a prolonged burst of tracer-rounds but ordinary ammo will just make a hole.

UNDER FIRE

Not that they ever hit him, but baddies tend to pour endless machine-gun fire on the hero. Most machine pistols fire between 700 and 950 rounds per minute and the magazines hold 30-35 rounds, so on continuous fire you're out of ammo in less than three seconds!

THE AMMO EXPLOSION

An ammunition store is set on fire and bullets scream out in all directions? No. Small-arms ammunition will rupture when burned but, without being confined to the chamber of a firearm, the actual bullet goes nowhere.

⁓

EXPLODING DYNAMITE

Dynamite is in fact extremely stable and needs a blasting cap to set it off. In small quantities you can set it on fire and it will burn like wood.

⁓

IN-FLIGHT ENTERTAINMENT

Although it makes for a good laugh to see the baddie sucked out through an airplane window that has been breached, this simply cannot happen.

⁓

DEATH BY BODY PAINT

In *Goldfinger*, a naked Shirley Eaton is killed with an all-body paint job, thus breathing new life into the old myth that anyone so treated will suffocate unless an area at the base of the spine is left uncoated. Frogs breathe through their skin; humans don't.

QUIZ 8

A What do calcium and potassium have in common?

B When a car veers to the left, are you thrown to the right?

C What are joined on a weather chart by isonephelic lines?

D Lord Byron's daughter worked on the development of which significant 'first'?

E What is the principal ore of aluminium?

F What do bromine and mercury have in common?

G Which law states that 'for every action there is an equal and opposite reaction'?

H What are dated by dendrochronology?

I Which extremely hard metal is also known as wolfram?

J Which alkaloid is present in cola drinks?

K What is measured by an anemometer?

L Which vitamin is also known as retinol?

M Which is the most abundant gas in the atmosphere?

N What is the purest form of carbon?

O Where in the bathroom would you most likely find titanium dioxide?

ANSWERS TO QUIZ 8
NOT SO EASY — YOU'LL NEED A MIRROR TO CHECK THESE OUT!

A   They are both metals, as indicated by the 'ium'.

B   No, you stay still while the car shifts left underneath you.

C   Areas of equal cloud cover.

D   She co-developed the first computer with Charles Babbage.

E   Bauxite.

F   Both are liquid at room temperature.

G   Newton's Third Law of Motion.

H   Trees.

I   Tungsten.

J   Caffeine.

K   Wind speed.

L   Vitamin A.

M   Nitrogen — about 78 per cent.

N   Graphite.

O   In your toothpaste — it is what makes it white!

SPACE: THE FINAL FRONTIER

THE SPACE RACE

OPERATION PAPERCLIP

After the Second World War, the Americans launched Operation Paperclip to 'hoover up' Nazi doctors and scientists, many of them war criminals condemned to death in absentia at Nuremberg. Having whitewashed them, they brought them home to set up the space programme.

త౪౦⊗

DR HUBERTUS STRUGHOLD

Dr Hubertus Strughold knew all about human reaction to vacuum, pressure and temperature extremes but there were red faces in NASA in 1958 when the public discovered Strughold had gained such knowledge experimenting on children in Dachau.

SS MAJOR WERNER VON BRAUN

Prime catch of Operation Paperclip was SS Major Werner von Braun. The Saturn rocket was a 'rebranding' of the A10 that von Braun had designed to strike New York. This was just one of many things kept secret by NASA, and 'Uncle' Walt Disney himself was hired to sell von Braun and his inventions to the American public. Inspired by the German sci-fi movies he had seen as a lad, von Braun instituted the reverse-count launch sequence to the Nazi rocket sites and brought the gimmick to America to create the sonorously voiced 'countdown'.

∽⊙⊚⊚∾

DEEP SPACE

First into deep space was the US Army. In 1957 someone forgot to remove the metal cover from the vent to an underground nuclear test in the Nevada Desert. Reviewing film of the cover 'going like a bat out of hell', astrophysicist Bob Brownlee calculated that it more than achieved escape velocity and might now be nearing Venus.

∽⊙⊚⊚∾

DID YOU KNOW?

Believe it or not, NASA now has a complete department working on the design and production of a *Star Trek*-style warp drive!

WHAT TO WEAR?

To achieve the necessary articulation, the designers of the first spacesuits visited the Tower of London in 1962 to base their design on an all-enclosing suit made for Henry VIII. In gratitude, one of the Apollo suits was sent to London in the 1970s so it could stand next to its inspiration. Oh, and they cost about $11 million each.

⌯⌯

FROM A HORSE'S ARSE TO THE MOON

Roman chariot makers worked on multiples of a unit equivalent to the average horse's backside to determine the axle-length for stability, and so forth. The two horse-arse axle width – equating to 4 feet 8.5 inches – became something of a standard. The Solid Rocket Boosters for the Space Shuttle were made in Utah and had to be transported out on a rail-line and through a tunnel that was only slightly wider than the track. So, it was the width of two horses arses that determined the size of those SBRs.

DID YOU KNOW?

When astronauts return from space they are about 2 inches taller. In the weightlessness of space the cartilaginous discs between the vertebrae in the spine expand, as indeed they do while you sleep on earth (we are all taller first thing in the morning).

FLYING SAUCERS

The term 'flying saucer' was coined in 1947 by American pilot Kenneth Arnold, who claimed he was passed by a group of UFOs that were shaped like 'giant saucers'.

❖

After UFO sightings hit the headlines, manufacturers churned out plastic 'flying saucers' in their millions. Today we call them Frisbees.

❖

About 2 million Americans have claimed abduction by aliens.

❖

The highest number of abduction claims per capita population comes from California.

❖

In America you can take out insurance against alien abduction for about $160 per year.

❖

The first to talk of green men seems to have been sci-fi writer Edgar Rice Burroughs in his *A Princess of Mars* (1917).

❖

The first country to show a flying saucer on its postage stamp was Equatorial Guinea in 1975.

SPACE ODDITIES

- Every hour, the universe expands over a billion miles in all directions.

- At the earth's core sits a massive and very solid iron-nickel ball about three-quarters of the size of the moon.

- Venus is the slowest-turning planet, taking 243 days to complete one rotation; the fastest is Jupiter with a ten-hour day. Pulsars are the speed-freaks of the universe, rotating up to 700 times a second.

- The sun is actually bright white and only shows yellow due to atmospheric pollution, which is also responsible for making the stars appear to 'twinkle'.

- There is no dark side of the moon. It is in a tidal lock with the earth so it always presents the same face to terrestrial observers.

DID YOU KNOW?

The only building visible from space is the ridiculously massive Romanian Parliament with a footprint of about 350,000 square miles.

DID YOU KNOW?

When NASA's *Skylab* broke up in 1979, some of the debris landed on the town of Esperance in Western Australia. The local council sent NASA a $400 littering fine, which was finally paid in 2009.

- We have all seen space cowboys taking a nail-biting ride through the asteroid belt but, in reality, the odds of hitting anything are astronomical. The gap between any two asteroids ranges from hundreds to thousands of miles.

- Only in sci-fi movies do black holes hoover up everything in their path. In reality, matter may fall into them but the black hole does not 'suck'.

- So called shooting stars or falling stars are just meteors and about 500 of them hit the earth every year.

- Some of the stars you 'see' in the sky imploded years ago but the light is still travelling towards earth. Conversely, there are new stars that you cannot see as the light has not got here yet.

DID YOU KNOW?

Light is not always the fastest thing in the universe; on the sun sound travels many times faster than light and, on earth, ultrasound is faster through water than light.

- Venus is the only planet that rotates clockwise.

- The sun travels round the galaxy once every 200 million years and it burns up 360 million tons of matter each year.

- In 2004 a new star, some 2,400 miles in diameter, was discovered to be made entirely of diamonds. The crystallized white dwarf was promptly named Lucy in reference to the Beatles' song. On Jupiter and Saturn it actually rains diamonds and in 5 billion years our sun will impact to a very, very large diamond.

- In 1781 William Herschel discovered a new planet, which he called George in honour of his patron, Mad King George III. It was renamed Uranus in 1850.

- Spinning at about 1,000 mph, the earth is also moving through space at 67,000 mph.

🧻 No one can belch in space as reduced gravity precludes the separation of gas in the stomach.

🧻 Neutron stars are so dense and have such gravitational pull that an object dropped just a metre from the surface would hit at about 7 million kph.

DID YOU KNOW?

The last man to walk on the moon was in 1972. Since then it has only been visited by unmanned vehicles.

FAMOUS UFO SPOTTERS

Billy Ray Cyrus

❖

Will Smith

❖

Russell Crowe

❖

Dan Aykroyd

❖

Mick Jagger

❖

John Lennon

❖

David Bowie

❖

Muhammad Ali

❖

William Shatner

❖

Ronald Reagan – twice!

DID YOU KNOW?

Any liquid expelled into space, such as astronauts' urine, will form itself into a sphere due to its surface tension.

ANIMALS IN SPACE

MEXICAN FRUIT FLIES

The first creatures to go into space were fruit flies sent up from White Sands, New Mexico in 1947 in a captured German V2 rocket to gauge the effects of radiation of living entities. All were recovered alive.

ເວົ້າຫວ

ALBERT THE MONKEY

In 1949 the Americans launched another V2 with Albert II, a rhesus monkey, the only passenger. Albert reached a height of 83 miles but did not survive his return as parachute-failure caused the disintegration of his capsule.

ເວົ້າຫວ

TSYGAN AND DEZIK

In 1951 the Soviets sent up two space dogs called Tsygan and Dezik into a suborbital flight. They became the first higher organisms to be successfully recovered from any mission.

ເວົ້າຫວ

LAIKA THE STREET DOG

Taken off the streets of Moscow at random, where she was reckoned to have already become accustomed to cold and hunger, Laika, a three-year-old mongrel, became the first creature to go into orbit and did so in 1957 on Sputnik 2. As was intended, she died in space as the technology to recover vehicles from orbit was yet to be developed.

⤞◈⤝

ABLE AND BAKER

In 1959 Able and Baker, a rhesus monkey and a Peruvian squirrel monkey respectively, went up in the nose cone of an American Jupiter rocket. Withstanding 40 G on their 10,000 mph re-entry, these two were the first primates to make it home from space alive.

⤞◈⤝

BELKA, STRELKA AND FRIENDS

In 1960 the Russians responded with Sputnik 5, which not only took aloft two dogs, Belka and Strelka, but also a rabbit, forty mice, two rats and fifteen flasks of fruit flies, all becoming the first creatures to go into orbit and come back alive. One of Strelka's puppies, Pushinka, was given to JFK's daughter, Caroline, by Khrushchev and, after a hot Cold War romance with another Kennedy canine called Charlie, their descendants are still in the Kennedy family today.

⤞◈⤝

HAM THE CHIMP

America struck back in 1961 with Ham the Chimp, who was trained to pull levers and flick switches for rewards. Wearing a specially designed spacesuit, Ham was sent into space in a Redstone rocket to become the first living creature to perform basic tasks in space. With Ham having proved that mental ability was not impaired in space, Alan Shepard made his historic flight three months later.

JELLYFISH AND A PREGNANT COCKROACH

From the 1960s onwards, both the USA and Russia sent into space everything from bullfrogs to jellyfish, the latter unfortunately returning without the ability to tell which way was up. And in 2007, the Russians sent aloft a pregnant cockroach called Hope, who became the first creature to give birth in space – all thirty-three of her offspring were pronounced normal on their return.

QUIZ 9

A   Most of the moons in the solar system are named after what?

B   The moons of Uranus are unique in that they are named after whose fictional characters?

C   Name the first satellite put into orbit in 1957.

D   What is an orrery?

E   In terms of space travel what is a perigee?

F   Name the first woman to go into space.

G   Which early astronomer wore a false nose and why?

H   Name the shuttle sent to fix the Hubble telescope in 1993.

I   By what name are the strata of radiation surrounding our planet known?

J   How many people have actually walked on the moon?

K   Which is the largest of the planets in our solar system?

L   Name the closest star to the earth.

M   As the earth shifts on its axis, Vega is due to replace Polaris in which role?

N   Name earth's largest satellite.

O   Name the only planet in the solar system not named after a god.

ANSWERS TO QUIZ 8

NOT SO EASY — YOU'LL NEED A MIRROR TO CHECK THESE OUT!

A Characters from Greco-Roman mythology.

B Characters from Shakespeare's plays.

C Sputnik 1.

D A mechanical model of the solar system.

E The point of a satellite's orbit closest to the earth.

F Valentina Tereshkova in 1963.

G Tycho Brahe; it was cut off in a duel so he wore stick-on noses.

H Endeavour.

I The Van Allen Belt.

J 12.

K Jupiter.

L The sun.

M The North Star.

N The moon.

O Earth.

THE DOCTOR WILL SEE YOU NOW: HEALTH, MEDICINE AND STRANGE EXITS

RARE MEDICAL CONDITIONS

PARRY-ROMBERG SYNDROME

Parry-Romberg Syndrome, also known as progressive hemi-facial atrophy, affects one side of the face only and, through neurological damage and tissue shrinkage, reduces that side of the face to something resembling a shrunken head while leaving the other side unaffected.

❧❧❧

CAPGRAS SYNDROME

Capgras Syndrome is the result of people suffering a minor impairment in the part of their brain responsible for recognizing faces. Sufferers become convinced that their nearest and dearest have all been replaced by almost lookalikes, as they increasingly perceive minor differences in their faces.

❧

MARY HART SYNDROME

Mary Hart Syndrome afflicts fans who become so obsessed with some celebrity or other that they lapse into hysterical fits, almost like an epileptic seizure, if so much as shown a photograph of their idol. It is named after American TV personality Mary Hart with whom the condition was first associated.

❧

LAUGHTER-INDUCED SYNCOPE

This affects those who enjoy their comedy to excess and laugh themselves into a near coma. More common than you would think, this is nicknamed Seinfeld Syndrome in America.

❧

DID YOU KNOW?

Men only have nipples because all foetuses start out female.

RAPUNZEL SYNDROME

Trichophagia, also known as Rapunzel Syndrome, besets those given to chewing the ends of their long hair. As hair cannot be digested, the consumed mass accumulates in the intestines, often needing surgical removal. The largest to date, a 4.5-kilo hairball, was removed from a teenage girl in Chicago in 2006.

DYSGEUSIA

Sometimes caused by drug abuse and sometimes a side effect of chemotherapy, dysgeusia is a scrambling of the ability to taste foods properly. For example, vinegar can taste excessively sweet to sufferers and chocolate acrid and bitter.

ALIEN HAND SYNDROME

Sometimes called Dr Strangelove Syndrome, after the character in the eponymous film who is unable to stop his right hand giving Nazi salutes, alien hand syndrome results in one hand reaching out to grab something leaving the sufferer no option but to use the other hand to restrain it.

DID YOU KNOW?

As well as having unique fingerprints, humans also have unique tongue prints.

FREGOLI SYNDROME

Named after an early twentieth-century Italian quick-change entertainer, Fregoli Syndrome can sometimes follow a serious blow to the head. Mercifully rare, the victim suddenly sees the face of someone they know changing to that of someone else, irrespective of gender.

❧

WEREWOLF SYNDROME

Although it is rare and usually genetic, Werewolf Syndrome, or hypertrichosis, results in the victim's body and face being covered with excess levels of hair. The condition can also be triggered by anorexia.

❧

FISH ODOUR SYNDROME

Those afflicted with Fish Odour Syndrome, or trimethylaminuria, emit an odour that resembles rotting fish. Of unknown cause, the condition usually asserts itself in childhood and worsens around puberty.

❧

AMAZING FACTS ABOUT THE HUMAN BODY

Each blood cell takes just over a minute to complete one full lap of the human body and will travel 1,000 miles in its lifespan.

❖

The brain is over 80 per cent water but can store 1,000 terabytes of information.

❖

In the adult body, 300 billion cells die and are replaced every day.

❖

The nose can 'remember' over 50,000 smells but it is women rather than men who have the better sense of smell overall.

❖

The largest organ in the body is the skin and the outer surface, which is actually dead material, completely renews on a twenty-seven-day cycle.

❖

Every step you take brings over 200 muscles into play.

❖

Stomach acid is strong enough to dissolve zinc and other metals – even razor blades.

❖

To save us the indignity of digesting ourselves, the stomach lining is constantly replacing itself at the rate of about 750,000 cells a minute.

❖

The liver is the only organ that can regenerate itself. From as little as 30 per cent of its original mass, given time, the liver can grow back to its normal size.

❖

The average human sheds about 500,000 skin particles every hour, which equates to about 150 lb in the average lifespan.

❖

The longer the finger, the faster the nail grows; no one knows why.

❖

Humans are born without kneecaps, which form when a child is about four.

DID YOU KNOW?

About 6 per cent of the global population have three nipples: Harry Styles, Mark Wahlberg, Tilda Swinton, Lily Allen and Carrie Underwood are all in the Triple-Nipple Club.

LOW CHOLESTEROL IS DANGEROUS! AND OTHER GOOD NEWS...

🧻 There is no such thing as the so-called tongue map, dividing the respective taste areas. All parts of the tongue can taste sweet, sour, whatever, with equal efficiency.

🧻 Low cholesterol has been linked to violent behaviour and suicide in a study of nearly 80,000 subjects, so lay off the statins and grab a doughnut.

🧻 It's a myth that you can die from lack of sleep in the short-term. For obvious reasons no one is sure of the limit, but it is thought to be in excess of two years.

🧻 Steroid abuse does not induce the penis shrinkage of popular myth, but apparently female bodybuilders experience considerable clitoral enlargement.

🧻 The heart never skips a beat. What is sometimes felt is better described as a double-beat or a beat of greater than normal force.

🧻 No one can develop resistance to antibiotics. It is the disease-inducing organisms themselves that develop resistance.

- The impact of most antibiotics is not impaired by drinking alcohol. This was a lie told to STD patients by doctors of the 1950s who were worried the infected person would be more likely to 'put it about' before being wholly cured if they were drunk.

- It is a myth that alcohol kills brain cells.

- There is no evidence linking stress to long-term hypertension. Those with stressful lives may embrace other factors – such as disrupted sleep patterns and drinking too much – but stress per se plays no direct part.

- Who invented the eight-glasses-of-water-a-day myth? No one knows, but it's rubbish.

DID YOU KNOW?

The average sneeze expels about 40,000 micro-droplets at about 200 mph, the cough expels about 3,000 micro-droplets at about 50 mph, and the poor old fart brings up the rear with an unimpressive 'muzzle-velocity' of about 30 mph.

OLD IS THE NEW NEW

Modern medicine has all too often scoffed at ancient remedies. Here are a few comeback kids from ancient medicine.

SOOTHING WILLOW BARK

The Greeks and Romans were using willow bark as a painkiller 2,500 years ago, much to the amusement of more recent medics. Until, that was, it was found to be a rich source of acetylsalicylic acid, which is now used to produce aspirin.

৫৩৬৯৩

GINGER

While modern medicine struggled to find a way to combat motion sickness and morning sickness, the ancients used simple extract of ginger, which is now recommended by doctors for both types of nausea and muscle cramps.

৫৩৬৯৩

NOT JUST FOR VAMPIRES

Throughout early Mediterranean cultures, garlic was widely valued for its medicinal properties and is now recognized as an effective treatment for mild hypertension, raised cholesterol and sinusitis. A daily dose is also seen as a cheap and effective way of preventing gastro-intestinal cancers and stroke.

৫৩৬৯৩

THE CLEANING POWER OF MAGGOTS

Maggots may not be the most appealing of creatures but, as they only eat rotten meat, they are making a comeback as a natural way of cleaning out infected wounds and ulcers. Just pop a few hungry maggots into an open sore and take them out when they have finished dining.

⌀

FRIENDLY BLOOD SUCKERS

Leeches are also making a welcome return. In reconstructive surgery the reattachment of veins can cause coagulation before blood flow has been established, so the little suckers are attached to the patient to drain excess blood from quite specific areas while their saliva works as a natural anti-coagulant.

⌀

SOLDIER ANTS

In South America the ancient native trick of using soldier ants in surgery is making a comeback in modern treatments when conventional sutures are thought to be impractical or inappropriate. Applied in a line along the wound, the ants are encouraged to bite with their considerable mandibles and so close the wound. The bodies are then cut off to leave the heads locked in place.

⌀

STEAM TREATMENT

Putting a tea towel over your head and leaning over a steaming bowl seems quite old-fashioned, but this simple form of steam treatment is still highly recommended for sinusitis and other forms of respiratory congestion.

COW'S BILE AND GARLIC

The ancient antiseptic recipe of cow's bile mixed with garlic that is left to brew for ten days was, in medieval times, recommended for styes and other skin infections such as leprosy. In March 2015 microbiologists at Nottingham University decided to give it a go and were surprised to find that it not only proved effective for styes but it also wiped out the new and deadly MRSA virus.

DID YOU KNOW?

Every year, about 2,000 left-handed people die in accidents caused by them trying to use equipment designed for right-handed people.

178

Toilet Trivia

More people in the world have access to mobile phones than working toilets.

10 STRANGE EXITS

1. In July 2013 a cow slipped off a cliff in Caratinga, Brazil, and fell through the roof of João de Souza's house, crushing him to death in his bed.

2. On 9 July 1993 lawyer Garry Hoy was keen to show prospective employees that the floor-to-ceiling windows of his twenty-fourth-floor complex in the Toronto Dominium Tower were quite safe. He flung himself enthusiastically against a pane, which promptly popped out of its frame, taking him to his death.

3. On 17 June 1871 American lawyer Clement Vallandigham was defending a client accused of murder by contending that the deceased could have gut-shot himself while drawing his own pistol from a kneeling position. Demonstrating his theory to the jury, Vallandigham gut-shot himself and, albeit posthumously, secured his client's acquittal.

4. On 25 January 1979, Ford Motor Company worker Robert Williams achieved the dubious honour of becoming the first person to be killed by a robot, which mistook his head for a component that needed bolting down.

5. Determined to prove his theory that yellow fever was transmitted by mosquito bites, in September 1900 American medical pioneer Jesse Lazear allowed himself to be bitten by infected insects. He was right, and died soon after.

6. Convinced he had designed the ultimate flying-suit-cum-parachute, on 4 February 1912 French tailor Franz Reichelt climbed to the top platform of the Eiffel Tower and donned his bat suit. Spectators and press said that he screamed all the way down.

7. Author of the Clayhanger series of novels, Arnold Bennett, mocked his fellow tourists in 1931 for their fear of drinking tap water in Paris. After quaffing a couple of glasses in derision of their concerns, he died of typhoid.

8. On 30 November 1958, *Armchair Theatre*
ran a live play in which the character played
by thirty-three-year-old Gareth Jones was
supposed to collapse with a heart attack.
When Jones collapsed for real from a fatal
heart-attack the cast, including Peter Bowles,
Donald Huston and Pauline Collins, just
carried on acting beside his dead body.

9. Just before the Battle of Spotsylvania in
the American Civil War, General John
Sedgwick mocked his men for cowering from
Confederate sniper fire by marching up and
down in front of them insisting that 'They
couldn't hit an elephant from...'

10. On 19 October 1988 the Montoya's pet poodle,
Cachi, fell from their thirteenth-floor balcony
in Buenos Aires to hit Martina Espina on
the head; both died. The nearby Edith Sola
stepped back in horror and was promptly run
over by a bus. A man in the gathering crowd
suffered a heart attack and fell into the street
where he was run over by an ambulance sent
to the scene.

YOU ARE WHAT YOU EAT?
FOOD MYTHS AND FACTS

Chocolate, pure and black, is not fattening.

❖

Apples, pears and plums are all members of the
rose family.

❖

Antifreeze is used in the production of some
toothpastes and to stop some ice creams from
freezing solid.

❖

The notion that it burns more calories to eat celery
than are ingested is pure nonsense.

❖

Given water, the average human can live about two
months without food.

❖

Honey is basically bees' vomit.

❖

Apples are 25 per cent air – that's why they float
for bobbing.

❖

Cucumber is 97 per cent water.

❖

DID YOU KNOW?

Kissing originated from mothers passing pre-chewed food to weaning offspring.

Also used in floor, shoe and car polish, carnauba wax is used to put the shine on wine gums.

❖

Castoreum, used as a substitute for vanilla flavouring, is squeezed out of beavers' anal glands.

❖

Used as a softening agent in commercial bread production, L-cysteine is made from human hair and duck feathers.

❖

A raisin dropped into champagne will continually rise and fall until the fizz runs out.

❖

A popular ice-cream flavour sold in Tokyo is raw horsemeat.

❖

Mashed up cochineal beetles are used to make a red food dye called carmine.

❖

The banana 'tree' is actually a very large herb and its fruit a very large berry.

❖

Imported from India and Pakistan, bone char from cattle skeletons is used to make sugar white.

❖

Only Coca-Cola is allowed to import coca, the source of cocaine, into the USA.

❖

Popular perception aside, pint-for-pint, draught Guinness has fewer calories than fresh orange juice.

❖

Lemons contain more sugar than strawberries.

❖

Strawberries and raspberries are not berries at all but aggregate fruits.

❖

The berry family includes the watermelon, avocado, coffee, grape and pumpkin.

POPCORN LUNG TO FIDDLER'S NECK: UNUSUAL HEALTH PROBLEMS

PARROT KEEPERS' FEVER

Those who work with or keep parrots as pets are open to Parrot Keepers' Fever, a condition caused by inhaling microscopic particles of the birds' droppings or skin. A pneumonic condition marked by nausea, joint pain and fatigue, bird lovers are left feeling as sick as a parrot.

෴

POPCORN LUNG

Caused by airborne contamination of diacetyl, the artificial butter flavouring, workers in popcorn factories are going down with what is being called Popcorn Lung. It may sound funny but it is a serious and irreversible condition to which consumers inhaling such contaminant on opening bags of microwaveable popcorn are also vulnerable. One consumer so afflicted in Colorado recently accepted a settlement of $7 million.

෴

CLARINETTIST'S TONGUE

Clarinettist's Tongue is a painful ulceration cause by allergic reaction to the rosin used to coat the cane reed in such instruments.

෴

FIDDLER'S NECK

Fiddler's Neck, otherwise known as the Violin Love Bite, starts as a red mark on the side of the neck, which can be caused by either continual compression and friction or allergic reaction to sweat, causing chemicals to leach out of the varnish on the violin. Left unaddressed, that initial spot can spread over the entire side of the neck to leave it with a hard and leathery texture.

JOGGER'S NIPPLE

Best to avoid loose fitting tops when out jogging if you wish to avoid Joggers' Nipple, which is caused by the incessant rubbing of the fabric on that area as you move. Also, male pavement pounders should wear supportive underwear to avoid intimate whiplash strain in another sensitive area.

BAGPIPE LUNG

Bagpipe Lung is caused by the fact that the inside of the sheepskin sack is coated during manufacture with honey to keep it supple and airtight. Add to this the piper's breath and you have a warm, moist environment ideal for the generation of spores that are then inhaled by the player.

CHIMNEY SWEEP'S SCROTUM

The first occupational condition to be diagnosed was Chimney Sweep's Scrotum, an unpleasant cancer caused by the build-up of soot in such areas. Although other forms of heating have caused a massive reduction in the condition, it does still occur.

GUITARIST'S NIPPLE

Others prone to friction damage are classical guitarists for who Guitarists' Nipple is most commonly induced by those who frequently hunch over their instrument. There is also Guitarists' Groin, a DVT in the upper thigh caused by the player leaning down on the instrument during play.

THE PRE-SEX HEADACHE

When women complain of a headache before bed, they could be telling the truth. Sexual Headache is no laughing matter and can start at the moment of initial arousal before building up to explosive pain in the head and neck on orgasm. Sometimes the headache is accompanied by violent sneezing, nicknamed Honeymoon Rhinitis, which only serves to increase the headache.

QUIZ 10

A   Sitting at rest, the body burns how many calories in an hour?

B   The human body is 68 per cent what?

C   Which part of your body completely renews itself every four days?

D   Which part of you is four times as long as you are tall?

E   Apart from fun, what do blondes have more of than other people?

F   Which part of you is a quarter of your length at birth but only one eighth of your adult height?

G   Which is the longest bone in the body?

H   One in a thousand babies is born with what?

I   Which of the main senses is significantly diminished by eating?

J   How many senses do humans have?

K   By the age of sixty, what have you lost half of?

L   Which part of you remains the same size from birth to death?

M   Helicobacter pylori bacteria cause which painful stomach condition?

N   Two per cent of your body weight is made up of what?

O   Which part of the polar bear will kill you if you eat it?

ANSWERS TO QUIZ 10 *NOT SO EASY — YOU'LL NEED A MIRROR TO CHECK THESE OUT!*

A   About seventy.

B   Water.

C   The stomach lining.

D   The small intestine, which can reach twenty-four feet in length.

E   Head follicles. Blondes have about 146,000 while the rest of us have about 100,000.

F   Your head.

G   The femur or thigh bone, always a quarter of your height.

H   One or more teeth.

I   Hearing.

J   Depending on how you count them, anything from sixteen to twenty-one. Apart from the obvious five, we can also sense things such as pressure, acceleration, heat, cold, hunger, thirst and time amongst other things.

K   Your taste buds. If it isn't food that doesn't taste like it used to – it's you!

L   Your eyes.

M   Ulcers; nothing to do with stress or spicy food.

N   Bacteria, both external and internal.

O   The liver – it is so rich in Vitamin A that it is lethal to humans.

SOURCES

The Guinness Book of Animal Facts and Feats (1982) by Gerald L. Wood.

The Guinness Book of Animal Records (1995) by Mark Carwardine.

An Underground Education (1997) by Richard Zacks.

Black's Medical Dictionary – 42nd Edition (2009) by Doctor Harvey Marcovitch.

Science Desk Reference (1995) by Patricia Barnes-Svarney.

The Handy Science Answer Book (1994) by the Carnegie Library of Pittsburgh.

The Straight Dope (all publications) by Cecil Adams.

The Cabinet of Curiosities (1991) by Simon Welfare and John Fairley.

Brewer's Cabinet of Curiosities (2006) by Ian Crofton.

The Mental Floss History of the World (2009) by Erik Sass and Steve Wiegand.

Mental Floss Present Forbidden Knowledge (2005) by Will Pearson, Mangesh Hattikudur and Elizabeth Hunt.